CHES

WALKS FOR MOTORISTS

James F. Edwards

★

30 Walks with sketch maps

COUNTRYSIDE BOOKS
NEWBURY, BERKSHIRE

*Countryside Books' walking guides cover most areas of England
and include the following series:*

County Rambles
Walks for Motorists
Exploring Long Distance Paths
Literary Walks
Pub Walks

A complete list is available from the publishers.

First published 1975
by Frederick Warne Ltd.
© James F. Edwards

Revised and updated edition published 1991
Revised and reprinted 1993
© James F. Edwards 1991, 1993

COUNTRYSIDE BOOKS
3 Catherine Road
Newbury, Berkshire

ISBN 1 85306 115 8

Cover photograph of Peckforton Castle
taken by Andy Williams
Sketch maps by the author

PUBLISHERS' NOTE

At the time of publication all footpaths used in these walks were designated
as official footpaths or rights of way, but it should be borne in mind that
diversion orders may be made from time to time.

Although every care has been taken in the preparation of this Guide, neither
the Author nor the Publisher can accept responsibility for those who stray
from the Rights of Way.

Typeset by Acorn Bookwork, Salisbury, Wiltshire
Produced through MRM Associates Ltd., Reading
Printed by J. W. Arrowsmith Ltd., Bristol

For my mother

Acknowledgements

Thanks are due to the staff of the Public Rights of Way Unit, Commerce House, Chester, and in particular Messrs G. E. Porter and M. J. Nutkins, for their helpful advice and invaluable assistance and route checking.

Contents

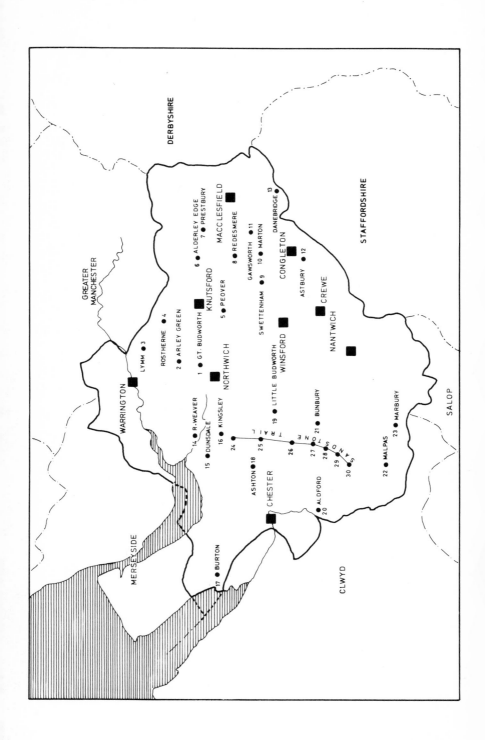

Introduction

Used to advantage, the motor car can propel the motorist to many interesting places; but it cannot go everywhere. Countless superb views, tiny hamlets and historical buildings which lie away from crowded main roads and motorways can only be reached using footpaths and bridleways.

This book will take you through a series of circular walks which begin and end at the car, along some of the more interesting footpaths and bridleways of Cheshire.

Cheshire is well known for its lush green fields, peaceful meres and well kept picturesque villages. Its churches, manor houses and ancient castles have always held great interest for students of history and architecture. This book attempts to combine all these facets to produce a varied and interesting series of walks.

Cheshire is also fortunate in that it has an abundance of quiet, virtually traffic free lanes. Many of these lanes have been used in the walks described in this book, not just as interconnecting links between footpaths, but in their own right, as a pleasant part of an overall circular route designed to give the walker variety during his jaunts in the countryside.

Between the hills of the Peak District National Park and the industrial towns of Northwich, Winsford, Crewe and Nantwich lies an area of rolling countryside where ancestral manor houses, waterside paths and quiet winding bridleways are to be found in abundance. To take a leisurely stroll through the area is to enjoy the peaceful atmosphere of rural Cheshire. The first 13 walks cover this area in detail.

From the cliffs behind Frodsham to the picturesque village of Marbury, from Northwich to the Welsh border, here is an area containing many varied and interesting walks. Ramble beside the Weaver and the Dee, pass through the historical township of Malpas, visit a host of scenic villages and lovely old churches. Once sampled it is an area to which you will return many times. Walks 14–23 cover this area in detail.

The 'Sandstone Trail' is a continuous footpath running from Frodsham to Whitchurch, by way of the Central Cheshire Sandstone Ridge. The trail passes along forest tracks at first, then crosses agricultural land to Beeston Castle. From here it climbs along a high ridge, where magnificent views of the surrounding countryside are to be seen. The trail is identified by way markers—small wooden squares engraved with a footprint containing the letter S, together with a directional arrow. Walks 24–30 enable you to complete a fair proportion of the trail in stages, by means of a series of circular walks.

The walks, which vary in length from two to seven miles, pass over varied terrain and can be enjoyed by all ages. If you are new to country walking, start with the shorter walks and build up to the longer ones. You will arrive back at the car having enjoyed an excursion into the countryside feeling refreshed in mind and body.

Rights of Way

All the routes described are on public rights of way, but footpaths can be legally re-routed due to land development or road alterations, in which case diversionary signs are usually shown by the Highway Authority.

If a right of way is obstructed, it would be helpful if details of the obstruction, together with its location, are reported to:

The Public Rights of Way Unit
Cheshire County Council
Commerce House
Hunter Street
Chester
CH1 2QP

Equipment

Footwear is all important. Waterproof walking shoes or boots are recommended, preferably worn over woollen socks. Smooth soled shoes should not be worn as they can cause accidents and make walking hard work, especially after wet weather.

Lightweight waterproof clothing should always be carried to combat the variable English weather.

A small rucksack can be useful to carry such items as food, cameras, binoculars and the like, which help to make a walk that much more enjoyable.

A note regarding maps and map references

The Ordnance Survey maps referred to at the beginning of each walk are the 1:50,000 Landranger Series. Three of these maps cover all the territory of the walks described in this book; these being maps 109, 117 and 118.

Although you should not encounter problems in finding where to park the car, the text of each walk does contain a grid reference giving the exact parking location.

The Country Code

The Country Code, as follows, makes sound common sense and should
be observed at all times:

Enjoy the countryside and respect its life and work
Guard against all risk of fire
Fasten all gates
Keep your dogs under close control
Keep to public paths across farmland
Use gates and stiles to cross fences, hedges and walls
Leave livestock, crops and machinery alone
Take your litter home
Help to keep all water clean
Protect wildlife, plants and trees
Take special care on country roads
Make no unnecessary noise

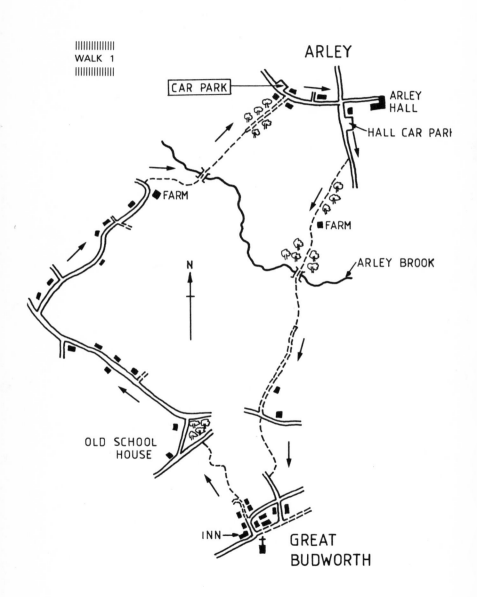

GREAT BUDWORTH

WALK 1

★

6 miles (9.5 km)

OS maps 109 and 118

One of Cheshire's choice villages, Great Budworth seems to possess that idyllic charm of a way of life long since gone. It has always been held in high esteem by those discerning enough to appreciate all that is best in Cheshire life, and many argue that it is Cheshire's loveliest village.

Park in the free car park at Arley, which is situated on the left hand side of the road prior to the entrance gate of Arley Estates. (Map ref. 670 810). Alternatively, you may wish to precede the walk with a visit to Arley Hall and its delightful gardens—in which case your starting point will be Arley Hall car park. (Map ref. 673 806). Arley is situated between the A559 road and the M6 motorway, 3 miles south of junction 20.

From the free car park turn left, go through the entrance gate of Arley Estates and turn right at the junction of lanes ahead. Walk down a straight lane for 500 metres, passing Arley Hall car park which is on your left, to where, on the right, there is a stile at the side of a field gate. (If you are starting the walk from Arley Hall car park a straight walk of 250 metres takes you to this stile.) Cross the stile and walk along the left hand edge of a field. Keep forward in the same direction and go over four further stiles, then enter a small wood via a gate. Follow a narrow path through the wood and go over a footbridge which passes over Arley Brook. Turn left, cross a stile into a field and keep straight ahead to emerge onto a concrete drive via a stile. A straight half mile leads to a road. Cross the road and enter a field over a small wooden stile in the opposite hedge. Keep forward with a fence on the immediate right and go over a stile at the far end of the field.

On a clear day the radio telescope at Jodrell Bank can be seen from here if one looks ahead and to the left.

Turn half right and cross the next field diagonally, in the direction of the church, then pass over a stile to enter a lane. Turn left, then go over a road to enter a gravel track. Proceed to a facing gate. Do not go through this gate, but turn right to follow a path between trees. Pass the school house on the right and the church on the left to join Church Street in the centre of Great Budworth village opposite the George and Dragon Inn.

The tower of the church was erected in 1520 and is a fine example of early Cheshire architecture, but the majority of the surrounding village houses were re-modelled during the nineteenth century.

Turn right along Church Street then bear left down Smithy Lane. The way becomes a grassy track and leads to facing gates. Go over the stile at the side of the gate on the right and walk forward keeping a hedge on your right. Pass over another stile, turn right and then left to follow the field edge, again keeping a hedge on your right. The path takes you to a stile on your right which is located at the left hand side of a field gate. On crossing this stile walk forward with a fence and trees on your left and after 50 metres bear left to shortly enter a hedged-in track via an old metal kissing gate. The track leads to a crossing lane. Go forward here down the opposite lane which is signposted to Antrobus and Warrington. Pass the Old School House and at the next junction turn left, again in the direction of Antrobus and Warrington.

Enter the hamlet of Antrobus and keep forward past Brook Cottage. Follow the roadside footpath and keep on past a turn-off to Northwich to shortly arrive at Hollins Lane. Enter this lane and continue in the direction of Crowley and Arley. Pass Grandsires Green Farm and keep on past Keepers Lane. Follow Hollins Lane for a further ½ mile to where, 150 metres after passing Hunters Moon Cottage, the lane turns sharply to the left. Leave the lane here and go over a facing stile at the side of a gate. Walk forward, skirting farm buildings, then turn right by a large barn. Follow a facing track keeping a hedge and fence on your immediate left and pass over two stiles which are set at the side of gates. Another stile on the left leads to a footbridge which passes over Arley Brook. Care is required here, as the passage of time has made the footbridge rather shaky. Keep forward across a facing field, go over a stile, and continue with a hedge now on your left. A further stile gives access to a track which is bounded on each side by tall trees. The track takes you past a dwelling and onto a crossing lane.

Turn left here and walk back to the car park which is on the right. (For Arley Hall car park, turn right, go through the entrance gate of Arley Estates and turn right at the junction of lanes ahead.)

ARLEY GREEN

WALK 2

★

4½ miles (7 km)

OS map 109

On the road between High Legh and Great Budworth and close to the M6 motorway is a roadside parking area adjacent to Litley Farm. (Map ref. 691 806).

Park here and proceed down a bridleway which is indicated by an interesting old sign which reads:

> This road forbidden is to ALL,
> Unless they wend their way to call,
> At mill or green or Arley Hall.

Another more modern and less interesting sign says: 'Private Road—Public Bridleway'.

Go forward, passing through a gate at the side of a lodge house and on down a wooded lane. Turn right just before the gate of a second lodge house and cross Arley Brook to enter the hamlet of Arley Green.

On the left across the green, and at the far side of a neat row of cottages, is the timber building of the old school house. One can well imagine the scene of years ago when the spring festival of May Day would be celebrated around a maypole set in the centre of the green.

Continue forward to pass an old water pump on the right, then look across to the left where there is a fine view of Arley Hall across the fields. The way now becomes cobbled for a short distance, this being part of the original road to the Hall. Keep forward past a lane on the right, and continue with trees on the left, to turn next right down a rough track. Pass a private road on the left, then leave the track to the right of a small bridge and go through a gate. From here follow the right hand side of a facing ditch for 200 metres, then go left over a footbridge and stile to enter a field. Turn right and keep forward to pass over a stile at the right hand side of a crossing hedge. After a short distance the fence on the right turns away to the right, but the footpath is diagonally left, to join a stile at the approach to a footbridge over the M6 motorway.

Cross the motorway, turn right, then keep right again to follow a lane past Arley View. Keep forward past dwellings on the left and turn right at the T junction ahead. This lane turns left shortly, but keep forward, passing to the right of Northwood Cottage and on past a private road to Northwood House, to arrive at a facing gate. Pass through this gate keeping forward with a hedge on the right and pass through a further two gates to reach another footbridge over the motorway.

13

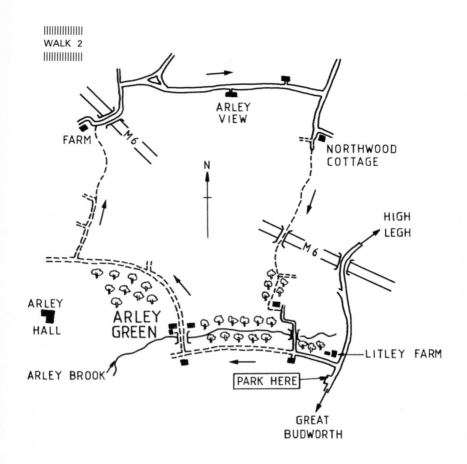

Cross the motorway, go through a gate, and follow a track straight ahead between trees to a facing gate. Do not go through this gate but take the path to the right which leads through woodland. Shortly, the path turns left to skirt around a group of cottages and leads onto a lane where the way is right. The lane takes you once again over Arley Brook. At the junction ahead turn left where a short stroll takes you back to the car.

LYMM

WALK 3

★

4½ miles (7 km)

OS map 109

Lymm is a watery place. The Bridgewater Canal skirts its north side, whilst to the south there is a dam, the outfall of which flows through the centre of the village.

This leisurely walk passes alongside these waterways and makes an ideal evening walk during the summer months when the days are long.

Park in the public car park situated on Pepper Street, close to the centre of the village of Lymm. (Map ref. 684 873).

On leaving the car park turn right and pass Lymm Cross, an old sandstone monument, then turn right again. Walk past The Golden Fleece Inn, then pass over a hump-backed bridge which takes you over the canal. Turn right now and walk along the canal tow path.

You are now walking alongside the famous canal that ushered in the canal age and, with it, the Industrial Revolution in Britain. The Bridgewater Canal was engineered by James Brindley to distribute coal from the Duke of Bridgewater's estates at Worsely near Manchester. The canal, which was completed in 1767, runs through Grappenhall to enter the Mersey through a series of locks at Runcorn.

Keep forward along the tow path for almost a mile and pass under two bridges. Shortly after the second bridge (Granthams) the canal passes over a lane. Descend some steps here to leave the canal side and walk under the bridge. Follow the lane and bear right to pass Warrington Lane. After 300 metres leave the lane and pass over a stile on the right which is situated at the side of a field gate. Walk forward, keeping a hedge on your immediate left. The path turns right, then left, past a deep-set pond and leads to a stile which gives access to a woodland path. Keep forward through the trees to shortly emerge into a field via a stile. Follow a field-side path which takes you towards a church spire which can be seen straight ahead.

In the distance Thelwall Viaduct can be seen carrying the M6 motorway over the Manchester Ship Canal.

Go over a stile and enter a lane. Turn left and pass the church, then turn right down a narrow fenced-in path which starts at the side of a field gate. Follow the path across the fields and turn right at the lane ahead. Shortly, there is a sports field on your right. At the next junction walk straight ahead to climb slightly between railings and proceed with a fence on the right and houses on the left. There is another sports field

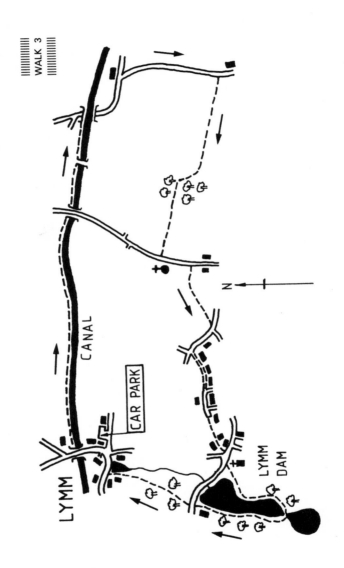

WALK 3

LYMM

CANAL

CAR PARK

LYMM DAM

N

on the right here. The path shortly joins a road where the way is right in the direction of St Mary's Church which can be seen straight ahead. Pass Greenwood Road and then continue to enter a fenced-in path between houses. Emerge onto a road opposite the church. Cross the road and follow a path which starts at the right hand side of the church grounds and leads to the water's edge of Lymm Dam.

Keep forward, staying close to the water's edge and go over some closely set stepping stones. After 100 metres climb up some steps on the left and proceed along higher ground. The path follows the contours of the dam then drops down to the right to take you over two small bridges in quick succession. The path climbs, turns to the right, and continues along the opposite side of the dam. The path passes close to the water's edge, where there is a nice view of the church across the water on the right. The path shortly meets a road where the way is straight ahead through a gap in a facing fence and down some steps, then along a pleasant pathway through overhanging trees to emerge onto the road in the centre of Lymm village.

The village, built on a huge undulating bed of sandstone rock, contains many interesting buildings and boasts five inns!

Turn right and follow the road which bears left, then climbs back to Lymm Cross and the car.

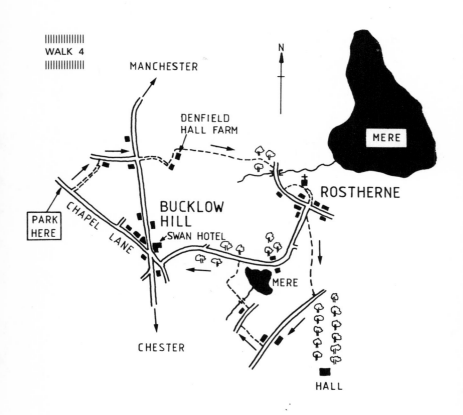

ROSTHERNE

WALK 4

★

3¾ miles (6 km)

OS map 109

Lying as it does, close to the conurbation of Greater Manchester, Rostherne is usually by-passed by those eager to search for something more distant, little realising that on their own doorstep is the very seclusion which they seek.

On the A556 road between the M6 and M56 motorways is the village of Bucklow Hill. Opposite the Swan Hotel is Chapel Lane. Drive down here for ⅓ mile and park on the grass verge at the side of the road. (Map ref. 726 836).

The footpath begins through a gateway on the right. There is a footpath sign here. Go forward along a field track keeping a hedge on the right, to emerge onto a crossing lane by the side of a cottage. Turn right and shortly cross the main road, then go forward down the entrance drive of Denfield Hall Farm. Pass through two gates, then turn left before the farmhouse to enter a field through a kissing gate. Bear right and go forward with a hedge on the right to keep in line with the church tower ahead. Pass through a second kissing gate and follow a path across the field towards the church. Go through a gap in a facing hedge and descend some steps to join a lane close to a bridge over a stream.

There are two particularly interesting views from here. Straight ahead Rostherne Mere can be seen. It is over 30 metres deep and is kept as a nature reserve. Over to the right at the top of the hill, with a commanding view of the surrounding countryside is Rostherne Church.

Cross the bridge and climb the hill to enter the church grounds through a most unusual revolving lych gate. The church has a sandstone tower (1742) which replaced the earlier steeple (1533) and contains the tombs of the Egerton family of Tatton Park.

Leave the church porch, bearing left along a path to pass through a gate onto a track. Go through two more gates and meet a crossing lane. The way is straight ahead down the opposite lane to where, after 150 metres there is a stile on the left at the side of a field gate. Cross the stile and turn half right to walk diagonally across the field corner to arrive at a kissing gate. The footpath is diagonally left across the facing field to another kissing gate. Pass through the kissing gate and head towards farm buildings across the field.

As the buildings are almost reached, Tatton Hall can be seen down an avenue of trees straight ahead.

Go through a gate and turn right along the road. Pass farm buildings on the left and Dale Cottage (1626) on the right. Turn right over a stile immediately after Dale Cottage and go forward with a hedge on the right. The hedge turns right shortly, but keep straight ahead to pass over a crossing fence then forward with a fence on the right. Cross a stile at the side of a facing field gate and walk forward across the field to arrive at a gate. Pass through this gate and turn right to follow a lane. Pass in front of a cottage, then turn left to descend and pass over a stream and stile. Climb, bearing right, and cross a stile at the side of a field gate. Keep forward with a hedge on the left then cross a stile in a facing fence.

Straight ahead, Rostherne Church tower can be seen amongst trees, whilst down to the right is a large mere which is a favourite haunt of local fishermen.

Turn right and descend close to the mere, then go over a stile to meet a lane. Turn left and follow the lane for almost ½ mile, turning right at the junction ahead to arrive at the Swan Hotel.

Cross the main road to proceed down Chapel Lane and back to the car.

PEOVER

WALK 5

★

6½ miles (10.5 km)

OS map 118

If it were possible for the walker of today to have carried out this walk 300 years ago, he would report very little change in the overall views which he saw, when comparing it with the present time.

Two miles south of Knutsford on the A50 road is a roadside parking area close to the entrance of Radbroke Hall. (Map ref. 763 754).

Park here, and walk south past the hall entrance, keeping forward to where the road bends sharply to the right, close to the Whipping Stocks Inn. A footpath sign directs you along a track which begins at the side of a lodge house. Pass through gates and keep forward along the track.

The area here was used as a hunting park in medieval times by the Lords of the Manor of Over Peover.

Pass through a gate at the side of a cattle-grid. Bear right now and follow a grassy track for 200 metres to pass over a stile which leads into a field on the right. Keep forward with a fence on the immediate left and cross over a stile on the left, just before trees are reached. Go forward and almost immediately turn right over another stile to enter a wood. Bear left through the trees and pass to the left of some outbuildings to arrive at Over Peover Church.

The church contains some fine relics and alabaster effigies of the Mainwaring family, the earliest of which dates from 1415.

Over the wall at the side of the church, Over Peover Hall can be seen. The original hall was constructed entirely of timber, but this was pulled down in 1585 and a new brick building constructed during the following two years.

On leaving the church grounds keep ahead to turn left and then forward, turning right and left past the old stables. These stables, erected in 1656, are constructed of carved Jacobean woodwork and have ornamental plaster ceilings.

At the junction with the lane ahead turn right and keep forward, passing to the left of St Anthony's Cottages. The lane now becomes a stony track and shortly turns sharp left, but the way is straight ahead through a gateway onto a woodland path. Keep forward to join a lane, and on passing Longlane Farm turn left at the junction with the road ahead.

Proceed forward and shortly after passing over a stream known as Peover Eye, the Drovers Arms Inn comes into view on the right. Pass

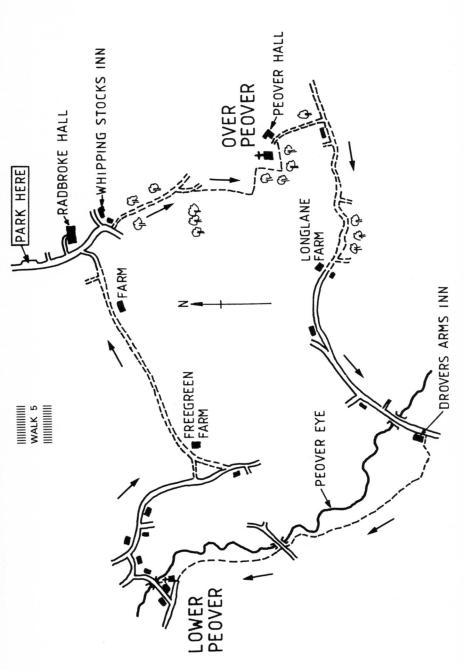

WALK 5

PARK HERE

RADBROKE HALL

WHIPPING STOCKS INN

OVER PEOVER

PEOVER HALL

FARM

N

LONGLANE FARM

FREEGREEN FARM

DROVERS ARMS INN

PEOVER EYE

LOWER PEOVER

22

the inn and go through a field gate on the right. Keep forward, then turn left to follow the edge of the field, and go through a gate in the hedge on the right. Cross a field to arrive at a facing gate. Do not go through this gate but go over a stile on the right, then almost immediately cross a fence which is set in a hedgerow. Turn left and proceed, keeping the hedgerow on your immediate left. Pass along three field edges then enter a large field. Keep forward along the left side of this field and pass close to farm buildings.

Keep forward then turn right at a facing hedge, to descend and turn left, through bushes, shortly before reaching Peover Eye. Follow the streamside path and go over a stile in a crossing fence. Continue along the streamside path and enter a lane through a gap in a facing hedgerow. Cross this lane and keep forward to once again follow a streamside path. The path shortly passes through a gap in a facing fence, where straight ahead across the meadow is the hamlet of Lower Peover, with its timbered church dominant.

The path keeps forward and then bears left to a gate at the left hand side of the church. Enter the church confines.

The churchyard contains the grave of Lord de Tabley, who was a local poet and naturalist. The church has an interesting exterior in that it is of timber construction but has a stone tower. Internally the church is filled with Jacobean furniture, including pulpit, stalls, screens and pews.

Surrounding the churchyard are both the old and modern school houses together with an inn 'The Bells of Peover' which has its own private gate into the churchyard.

Leave the churchyard and pass between the schoolhouses to proceed down a cobbled lane. Turn next right and pass the inn, then keep straight ahead to cross Peover Eye. Climb slightly and turn right at the junction ahead. Keep forward bearing right and on down Free Green Lane to bear next left. Shortly after passing Free Green Farm entrance turn left, opposite Free Green Cottage, and proceed down a bridle track. This track passes in front of Free Green Farmhouse, goes through a gate and continues through farm outbuildings. Keep forward along the track and go through two more gates then pass Sandylane Farm on the right.

Shortly the main road is met, where the way is left and back to the car park.

ALDERLEY EDGE

WALK 6

★

5 miles (8 km)

OS map 118

The hill at Alderley Edge is the first prominent landmark due south of Manchester, and this walk takes you close to its summit, where fine views of the surrounding countryside can be seen.

Leave the car on the large public car park which is close to the Wizard Restaurant on the B5087 road, a mile to the south-east of Alderley Edge village. (Map ref. 860 772).

Enter a track which commences at the side of the restaurant. Follow the track straight ahead and pass the Forester's Lodge.

The area around here is riddled with old mine workings, where copper and lead were dug out by early inhabitants and later under the watchful eyes of their Roman masters.

Follow the main track as it turns sharply to the right near tall scotch pines. Pass Edge House Cottage, then enter a path at the right hand side of the entrance to Edge House Farm. Cross two stiles and keep forward along a fenced-in path. Keep forward over two more stiles and on past Ridgeways Farm, to meet a crossing road where the way is forward to enter trees. Follow a path through the trees and turn right at the lane ahead. Pass stables, and where the lane turns sharp right keep forward, down the approach track of Finlow Hill Farm. Go over a stile on the right at the side of a large tree before the farm buildings are reached. Turn left, and keep forward with a fence on the left, to go over a stile at the left hand side of a wood.

Skirt around the wood, keeping a fence at your right side, then turn left at a crossing fence. Descend slightly, keeping the fence on your immediate right and cross two stiles in quick succession at the side of Hayman's Farm. Walk forward, keeping parallel with the farm approach track, and go over a stile at the side of a facing gate. Turn right and proceed along a track. Pass an attractive isolated dwelling and then turn left at the junction ahead.

You are now on Bradford Lane. The way is cobbled and straight and leads to a junction with the main road ahead. Turn left, and follow the roadside footpath past Sand Lane to arrive at the old mill of Nether Alderley.

The mill, which is open to the public, has been restored to its original working order, and a look inside should not be missed.

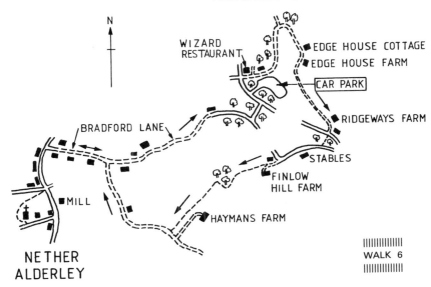

ALDERLEY EDGE

N

WIZARD RESTAURANT

EDGE HOUSE COTTAGE
EDGE HOUSE FARM

CAR PARK

RIDGEWAYS FARM

BRADFORD LANE

STABLES

FINLOW HILL FARM

MILL

HAYMANS FARM

||||||||||||||
WALK 6
||||||||||||||

**NETHER
ALDERLEY**

Cross the road from the mill and walk down a short lane which takes you to the church. Enter the church grounds and pass the splendid building of the old school house to go over two stiles at the left rear side of the church. A short forward stroll leads to a junction of paths at a gate. Go through the gate, cross a stream, turn right and walk across a field to arrive at the head of Sand Lane via a stile and gate.

Walk back and re-enter Bradford Lane. Keep left along the cobbles where the lane forks, and climb steadily past Bradford Lane Farm and Bradford House Farm. Keep forward, pass Bradford Lodge, then turn left at the junction ahead. A short stretch of level lane takes you to a T junction.

Turn left here and cross the road to arrive back at the car park.

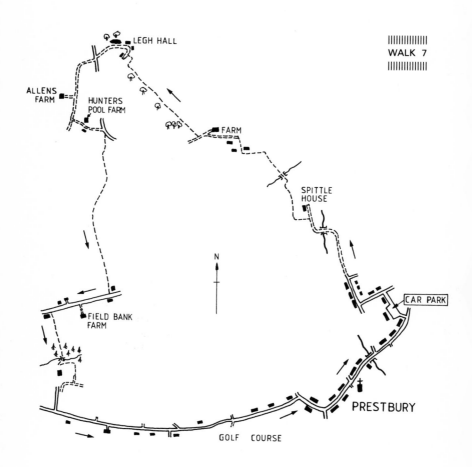

PRESTBURY

WALK 7

★

5 miles (8 km)

OS map 118

Prestbury has much to interest the inquiring visitor. The village, which is bisected by the infant river Bollin, lies in a pleasant area of countryside north of Macclesfield and is near the junction of the A538 and A523 roads.

There is a public car park on the north side of the village, close to Pearl Street. Park the car here. (Map ref. 902 772).

Leave the car park in the direction of the way out sign. Turn left, and then right to proceed along Bollin Grove. Keep forward and enter a track which skirts to the right of a sports field. The track shortly turns left to a bridge over the river Bollin. Cross the bridge and go over a stile at the side of a facing gate. Follow the track as it turns to the right and go over a stile on the left just before a private drive to Spittle House. Walk forward and keep right to follow a path which takes you around the grounds of Spittle House, and go over a stile in a crossing hedge. Proceed, keeping a fence on your right and go over another stile near the field corner. The path quickly turns to the left and takes you down steps and over a footbridge. Climb forward, bearing left, and cross two stiles in quick succession. Continue, with a fence on your left. There is a stile on the left shortly at the side of a field gate. Cross this stile and continue with a fence now on your right.

A stile at the field corner leads you onto a track between a barn and a building. The track turns left and climbs past a farm outbuilding. Go over a stile at the side of a facing gate and cross a farm approach track to a stile in the opposite hedge where a sign points to Mottram St Andrew. On crossing this stile keep forward and descend across rough open ground, then cross a small footbridge, and climb forward. Keep forward along a field edge and continue past a path on the left which goes to Prestbury Road. Go over a stile in a crossing fence, climb, then turn right on meeting a facing hedge. Follow this hedge to arrive at a kissing gate which is set at the left hand side of a metal field gate.

Looking to the west from here, and if the day is clear, you should be able to make out the beehive shape of White Nancy, a monument which sits atop a hill close to Bollington.

Go through the kissing gate, turn right, and follow a cobbled track between a dwelling and outbuildings. The track bears left shortly, towards Wilmslow Road, and passes Legh Old Hall and the fine

27

Georgian building of Legh Hall. Pass a pool on the right to shortly arrive at a crossing road. Turn left, then immediately right, to enter a track. The track descends, turning left. The track takes you past the entrance drive of Allens Farm and continues to Hunters Pool Farm which sits on a rise on the left. Pass through the farm entrance gate. Cross the farmyard and go through a second gate. Walk forward along a macadam drive which climbs to meet a crossing road. Turn right and after 30 metres go over a stile on the right.

Walk to a stile which can be seen straight ahead at the left hand side of a facing gate. There is a small pond on the left now. Keep forward in the same general direction as before and walk across a large field in the direction of dwellings which can be seen straight ahead across the field. Go over a double stile in a crossing fence. Proceed with a hedge on the left now, then cross a stile to enter a lane. Turn right. Follow the lane past Field Bank Farm and after 300 metres go over a stile on the left, just before a dwelling is reached. Follow a field edge with a fence and the dwelling on your immediate right to quickly cross a second stile. Proceed, with a fence now on your left. Descend, then enter a small wood via a stile. Descend steps, cross a stream, and climb. Turn sharp left halfway up the climb and walk through trees to shortly arrive at a stile up some steps on the right. Cross the stile and emerge from the trees to enter a field.

Keep forward now with a fence on your right and join a facing track which quickly takes you through a kissing gate at the right hand side of a field gate. Turn right and climb along the track, then go through a small wooden gate on your right. Turn left and walk along a macadam drive which takes you onto a crossing lane. Turn left. Descend past the splendid black and white building of Normans Hall. Follow the lane for a further ¾ mile and pass the golf course to arrive at a T junction. Turn right, then left to enter the village of Prestbury.

On the left is the Legh Arms, once known as the 'Black Boy'. An inn has stood on this site since 1403. Keep forward past well kept shops, many of which have mullioned windows. Opposite the church there is a fine old black and white timber building which has been extensively restored and is now used as a bank.

Continue past the Bridge Hotel, cross the river Bollin, and keep on past the Admiral Rodney Inn to arrive back at the car park.

REDESMERE

6 miles (9.5 km)

OS map 118

A distinctive feature of the Cheshire countryside is the number of lakes or 'meres' which are to be found in abundance throughout the county. Several of these are quite large, as at Redesmere, near Capesthorne Hall, and part of this walk skirts alongside its eastern shore.

Drive down Fanshawe Lane, which joins the A34 road ¼ mile north of its junction with the B5392, and leave the car on the long narrow parking area at the head of Redesmere Lake. (Map ref. 849 713).

Walk back to the main road and turn left, then left again, to arrive at Siddington Church. Walk up the drive to the church, where some time should be spent in surveying this fine old building and its contents.

The church, consecrated in 1521, consists of a timber frame with wattle and daub filling. A leaflet relating its history, together with a description of its contents is available inside.

From the church porch proceed down a facing path and enter a field through a gate. Go straight ahead, and cross three fields and three stiles. After crossing the third stile keep forward with a fence on the left and then descend slightly to turn right by a small pond. Continue with a grassy bank on the left and climb slightly, bearing left, to cross a fence on the left some 25 metres before the field corner is reached. Skirt to the left of some facing trees, keeping forward with a field fence on the left, in the direction of farm buildings ahead. Go over a stile in the fence on your left which is 25 metres before a facing gate which leads into the farmyard. Follow a short length of fence as it turns to the right and arrive at a well defined track which leads away from the farm. Turn left along this track and walk away from the farm. Follow this track for almost ¾ mile, passing through four gates, to join a crossing lane, where the way is left.

After ¼ mile there is a wood on the left, with a track just before it, and a signboard indicating Crabtree Moss Farm. Follow this track and proceed through the farmyard. Go through a gate at the rear of outbuildings and enter a field. Keep forward for 50 metres, with a hedge on your left, then turn right to follow a well defined track. The track takes you through two gates and dips and climbs through trees. Arrive at Henshaw Hall Farm. After passing the farmhouse turn right to pass between the main farm buildings and outbuildings and walk forward to join a macadam drive. Pass a couple of dwellings and arrive at a

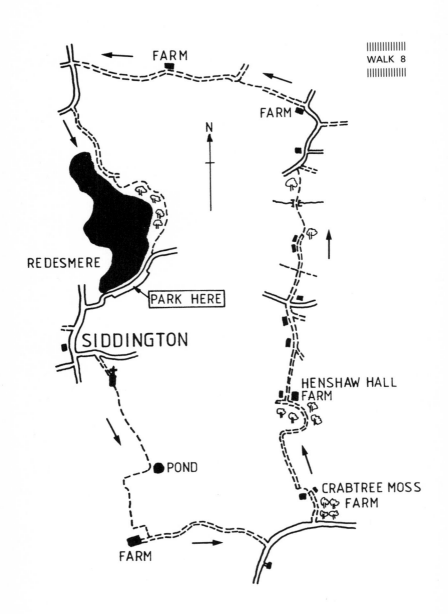

FARM

FARM

FARM

N

REDESMERE

PARK HERE

SIDDINGTON

HENSHAW HALL
FARM

POND

CRABTREE MOSS
FARM

FARM

crossing road. Go straight across this road and enter a facing track which commences at the left hand side of a dwelling. Climb steadily. The way takes you past the right hand side of two dwellings and becomes a grassy track. Shortly after passing the second dwelling go through a gate and walk forward with trees on both sides. Go over a stile and enter a large sloping field.

Keep forward and descend to a crossing fence which can be seen at the bottom of the slope straight ahead. Cross a stile in the fence, go over Fanshawe Brook via a footbridge, and quickly pass over a second stile. Climb forward with a hedge on the left, then pass close to outbuildings. A further stile gives access to a lane. There is a farm approach track on the right here but keep right to follow the lane. Pass a lane which shortly goes off to the right. There is an attractive dwelling on the left here with particularly well kept gardens.

After ¼ mile you will arrive at a farm on your left. Leave the lane here and enter a rough track which commences at the right hand side of the farmhouse. Go over a stile by a gate close to a large barn and continue with a hedge on your right. Cross two more stiles at the side of gates and enter a fenced in track. There is a track to the right here which leads to a farm, but keep forward here. On passing a small farm the way becomes a macadam lane. A straight ½ mile leads to the main road opposite an entrance to Capesthorne Hall.

Turn left and continue to where the road bends to the right. Go through a gate on the left here and follow a track. Quickly pass through a second gate and continue along the eastern shore of Redesmere, where there are pleasant views across the water. Leave the track, pass close to the Sailing Club, and go through a facing gate to follow a path through trees. The path takes you over a footbridge. After a further 70 metres go over a stile on the right which leads into a field. Keep forward with a fence and trees on your immediate right and cross two fields and two stiles to enter a lane.

Turn right and walk back to the car which is parked a short distance away at the head of Redesmere Lake.

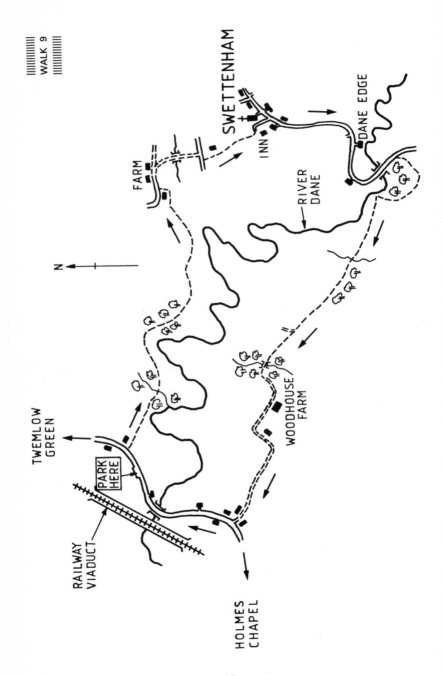

WALK 9

SWETTENHAM

DANE EDGE

INN

RIVER DANE

FARM

N

TWEMLOW GREEN

PARK HERE

RAILWAY VIADUCT

WOODHOUSE FARM

HOLMES CHAPEL

SWETTENHAM

WALK 9

★

5½ miles (9 km)

OS map 118

Swettenham is a place little visited. This is because it lies off the beaten track down a no-through-road and is, in the main, frequented only by local people. This isolation has resulted in a village where the hurly-burly of modern life seems 100 years away.

The walk commences near Holmes Chapel and never ventures far away from the winding river Dane.

The A535 road connects Holmes Chapel with Twemlow Green, Jodrell Bank and Chelford. One mile from the centre of Holmes Chapel the road descends and passes over the river Dane close to a large railway viaduct. A little further on there is a parking area on the left hand side of the road. This parking area is 100 metres before a footpath sign on the right which points to Swettenham. (Map ref. 776 679).

Leave the car, cross the road, and go over a stile where the footpath sign points to Swettenham. Walk forward to cross a large undulating field. Gradually bear left and converge with a hedge on the left to go over a stile at the side of a facing gate. Keep straight ahead along fairly level ground with the river on your right, and go through a gate which leads into trees. Descend through the trees, cross a stream, climb and go through a gate to enter a large sloping field. Bear right and walk forward, climbing slightly at first, to continue with trees on your immediate right. Where the trees finish bear left and climb across open ground to arrive at a stile at the right hand side of a field gate. Cross the stile and continue with a fence on the left and trees on the right.

The path shortly turns right, away from the fence, and drops down between trees. Go through a facing gate to emerge from the trees, cross a stream, and climb up a facing bank. Continue and pass through a gate in a crossing hedge. Pass close to a small pond then bear left to climb to the left of a wooded hill keeping the trees and a fence on your immediate right. On reaching more level ground walk forward, still with the trees and fence on your right, and go through a facing field gate. Continue along the higher ground with a fence now on your left. The path runs along the top of a rough grassy bank.

The view from here is particularly rewarding. Over to the right can be seen the hill at Mow Cop, whilst in the near foreground is the river Dane winding slowly westwards on its journey to Holmes Chapel and beyond.

Continue and pass to the right of farm outbuildings. Go through a gate then turn left to go over a stile which leads onto a lane. Turn right, pass close to a farm house, and on through two gates to follow a grassy track straight ahead. Shortly, the track forks close to a large dwelling on the left. Enter the right fork and descend through trees. Go over a bridge which takes you over Midge Brook and climb to a crossing lane. Turn right and after 20 metres leave the lane to the left and pass through a small gate. Quickly cross a stile close to outbuildings and walk forward along a field edge keeping a fence on your left. There is a large black and white detached dwelling on the left now. Go over a stile at the left hand side of a tall row of evergreen trees and walk forward to arrive at the church in the centre of the quiet village of Swettenham.

Turn right and pass between the church and an inn on the right called the Swettenham Arms. Arrive at a crossing lane and turn right. Follow the lane past Swettenham Cemetery, and a large house called Dane Edge. Continue, then go through a gate at the side of a house which takes you onto a track. The track leads to a bridge over the river Dane.

This is a pleasant spot. Fishermen will journey for miles to have an opportunity to pit their skills against the lively trout which abound in these waters.

Cross the bridge and continue along the track for a further 150 metres. Turn right now and climb up a grassy bank on your right keeping a fence and trees on your immediate right. Near the top of the climb go over a stile on the right, which takes you into the trees. The path winds through trees and banks of ferns then emerges into a field on the left. Follow the field edge for 150 metres then enter the trees on your right again to follow a descending path. Cross a stile which takes you into a rough, low lying, field. Bear left, then walk forward keeping a fence and trees on your left. Pass close to the river and continue, keeping to the centre of the level ground ahead. Go over a crossing stream via a plank. This crossing place is close to a confluence of minor streams. Climb up a facing bank and go over a stile in a crossing fence. Bear slightly right, and walk forward, to converge with a field fence. Proceed, keeping the fence on your immediate right. There is a large sloping bank on your left here. Go through a facing gate, cross a concrete drive, then immediately pass through a second gate to continue in the same general direction as before. Continue, with trees and a fence on your left. Arrive at facing trees. Turn right and after 80 metres arrive at a stile which leads into the trees. A footbridge takes you over a crossing stream. Emerge from the trees over a stile and turn left to join an uphill track via a stile at the side of a gate. The track turns to the right and leads past Woodhouse Farm. Follow the track as it turns left and right past a dwelling called Ryecroft, then keep straight ahead for ½ mile to emerge onto the Holmes Chapel to Twemlow Green road.

Turn right and after ½ mile arrive back at the car.

MARTON

WALK 10

★

4½ miles (7 km)

OS map 118

Marton lies in the midst of the rolling plains of south-east Cheshire. This is rich farming country, well known for its dairy produce, and to wander through the area gives a feeling of being close to the grass roots of life, far removed from the hurly-burly of city life.

Drive down Cockmoss Lane, ½ mile south of Marton off the A34 road. The lane is headed by a sign which says 'North Rode 3 miles'. Park the car on the wide grass verge on the left hand side of the lane close to where there is a stile, and a footpath sign which points to Marton. (Map ref. 853 675).

Leave the car and go over the stile, then bear diagonally left across a field to pass to the right of a facing hedgerow. Proceed with a hedge containing a row of telegraph poles on your immediate left. Cross a stile in a facing hedge then turn left and right to pass close to a barn. Walk down a short length of driveway which takes you to a road. Turn right and walk up to Marton Church.

The church is only small but it is quite rightly described as 'one of the ecclesiastical gems of Cheshire', and surely must be one of the finest timber churches in England. The unusually shaped tower and bell chamber are covered with wooden 'slates', and externally the whole building has that sense of proportion and charm which typified a bygone age. Founded in 1343, it contains some interesting fresco work and paintings, together with two old stone effigies reputed to be those of Sir John de Davenport and his son.

Leave the church and cross the road to go over a stile where a sign indicates Swettenham. Keep forward across a facing field then continue with a hedge on the immediate right. Cross two further stiles to enter a lane. Turn right here and follow the lane as it winds past a farm and an old black and white cottage. On meeting a crossing road keep forward where a sign says 'Gawsworth 3 miles'. Continue past Oak Lane and the primary school and keep forward for ½ mile to arrive at Pikelow Farm on the right. Pass the farm, and after a further 150 metres turn right to enter a track which leads to Marton Heath. Over to the right is a large lake which is reputed to be full of trout.

The track proceeds through woods. Keep forward past a cottage and follow the track across farmland where there are long views in all directions. Pass through three gates and climb up to Tidnock Farm.

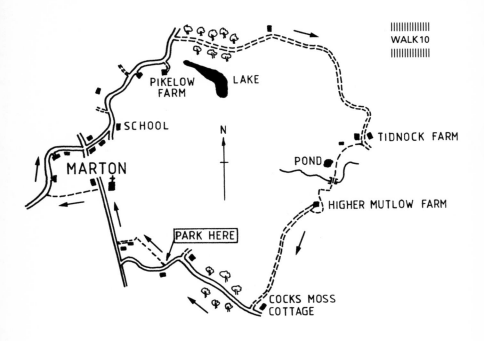

Bear diagonally right, go through a gate, and cross the farmyard to continue through another gate and onto a facing track. After 40 metres arrive at a facing gate. Do not go through this gate but turn right through a gate to enter a sloping field. Walk forward, along level ground at first, passing to the left of an old outbuilding. Bear left now and descend along an old half-hidden track.

This is the course of the old pack road between Macclesfield and Congleton which was in use up to the end of the last century.

Pass between a stream and a pond, then go over a footbridge on the left which takes you over the stream. Continue with a line of trees on the immediate right and go over a stile on the right which is at the side of a field gate. Walk forward along the lower ground, keeping a fence on your right. Shortly, Higher Mutlow Farm can be seen on a rise at the left. Arrive at a facing field gate. Do not go through this gate but climb to the left and go over a stile at the left hand side of the farm. Walk forward, keeping a hedge on your right, then turn right through a field

36

gate. Go over a stile and turn left along a track which leads away from the farm. Follow this well defined track for ½ mile, passing over five cattle-grids, to emerge onto a lane close to Cocks Moss Cottage.

Turn right, follow the lane through trees, bear left and shortly arrive back at the car which is parked on the right.

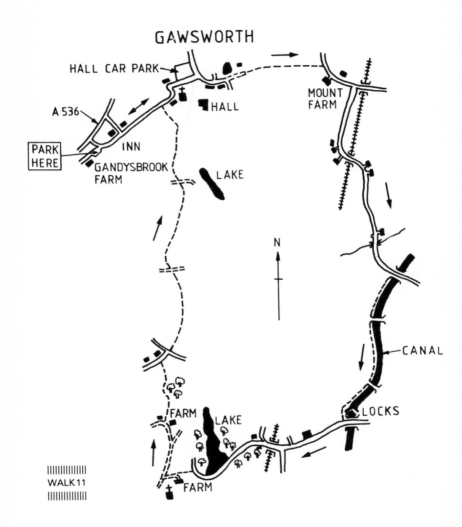

GAWSWORTH

HALL CAR PARK

A 536

PARK HERE

INN

GANDYSBROOK FARM

HALL

LAKE

MOUNT FARM

N

CANAL

LOCKS

FARM

LAKE

FARM

WALK 11

38

GAWSWORTH

WALK 11

★

6 miles (9.5 km)

OS map 118

This walk contains all the best ingredients of the Cheshire countryside—leafy lanes, field paths, a canal path, woodlands, lakeside paths, a lovely medieval church and a fine old manor house. All this, combined with views over to the rolling foothills of the Peak District National Park, make this walk one of infinite variety.

Gawsworth lies 3 miles to the south-west of Macclesfield just off the A536 road. You may wish to precede the walk with a visit to Gawsworth Hall—in which case leave the car on the large car park which is specifically for visitors. (Map ref. 891 698). If you are not visiting the hall, or if the hall is closed, there is a parking lay-by half a mile to the south-west, close to where a secondary road turns to join the A536. This parking lay-by is close to Gandysbrook Farm. (Map ref. 886 692).

From the car park near Gandysbrook Farm, follow the roadside footpath and walk towards Gawsworth Church. Pass the Harrington Arms Inn and then follow the road as it turns left and right past the church. There is a lake on the right now across which Gawsworth New Hall can be seen. Turn next right and enter the entrance lane to the hall. There are lakes on both sides here. (This is the point at which visitors to the hall will commence the walk.)

Walk past a large statue of Peel on the left and continue past charming mews cottages. Shortly after passing Gawsworth Court the lane turns right, but keep straight ahead along a short section of track to go over a stile at the side of a field gate close to a dwelling on the left called The Pigeon House. Keep forward with a hedge on your right and cross four fields, via stiles and gates, to emerge onto a crossing lane. Turn right and pass Mount Farm, then right again just before a railway bridge to proceed down Cowbrook Lane. The lane passes over the railway, then drops down over Cow Brook to climb to a bridge which passes over the Macclesfield Canal. Do not pass over this bridge, but go down steps on the left to join the canal tow path. Turn right and walk under the bridge (No. 51). Continue along the canal tow path and pass under two further bridges (Nos. 52 and 53) to arrive at Bosley Top Lock.

An interesting five minutes can be spent here, watching the boats as they pass through the lock.

Leave the canal tow path now, to the right of Bridge 54, and join a lane where the way is right. Shortly, the lane turns sharply to the right after passing over the railway, but the way is straight ahead through lodge gates to the left of Gateway Cottage. Follow a lane through trees and after ¼ mile skirt the edge of a lake.

The lake and surrounding trees are kept as a bird sanctuary, and many differing species may be seen.

The lane gradually climbs now, and leads to a cattle grid. Do not go over this cattle grid, but leave the lane to the left and go over a stile at the side of a gate. Follow a facing grassy path, keeping parallel to a fence on the left, then go over a stile in a crossing fence. There is a farm on the left here. Walk forward along a facing track, but after 50 metres turn sharply to the right over a cattle grid and continue along a concrete drive. The drive gradually climbs and then descends. Keep to the left where the way forks and continue to pass over a cattle grid at the side of a farmhouse. Keep forward and go over a stile at the side of a facing gate to enter a field. Cross the field and go over a stile at the left hand side of a small wood. Proceed forward along a rough grassy track with a fence, then a hedge, on your immediate left. A further stile takes you onto a lane. Turn right, and at the T junction ahead keep forward to cross a stile at the side of a facing gate.

Go forward climbing slightly, with a fence on the left, to cross two fields and two stiles. After the second stile go straight over a rough crossing track and pass over a stile at the side of a gate. Keep forward here, with a hedge on the left, to a stile in a crossing fence one field's length away.

One mile straight ahead Gawsworth Church can be seen, sited proudly on elevated ground.

Keep forward now in the general direction of the church, crossing three more fields and three stiles. Go over a crossing track—there is a lake over to the right here. Continue, and pass over three more stiles, to enter the last field prior to the church.

The view of the church across the field here is really splendid, and is a view which must have changed little since the church was built.

The path bears slightly left now to skirt the edge of the field. Proceed keeping a hedge on your left then go over a stile and down steps to enter a lane.

If you have parked the car near to Gandysbrook Farm the way is left to retrace your steps back to the car park. Before heading back to the car however, have a look around the church. Turn right and climb steps at the side of Gawsworth Rectory to enter the confines of the Parish Church of St James.

The walls and the roof of the church are over 500 years old, and the church stands on the site of a Norman chapel. The tombs and effigies of four generations of the Fitton family can be seen inside, the oldest of which dates from 1608. A leaflet describing points of interest for visitors is available inside the church.

If you have left the car at Gawsworth Hall car park leave the church on the north side and pass through a lychgate. Turn right. There is a lake on the right here across which Gawsworth New Hall can be seen. This view is at its best in early summer when the rhododendrons and lakeside iris are in full bloom.

A gentle stroll leads back to the car.

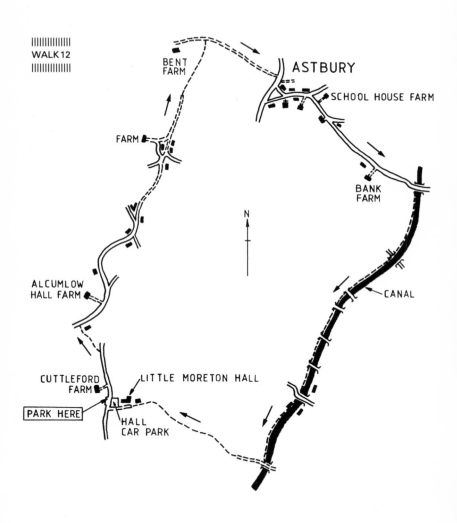

WALK 12

BENT FARM

ASTBURY

SCHOOL HOUSE FARM

FARM

BANK FARM

N

ALCUMLOW HALL FARM

CANAL

CUTTLEFORD FARM

LITTLE MORETON HALL

PARK HERE

HALL CAR PARK

ASTBURY

★

6¼ miles (10 km)

OS map 118

Some of the oldest relics of Cheshire man have been found in the Astbury area. A stone hammer dating from the Neolithic Age has been found at Moreton, and Bronze Age implements at Congleton. There are also traces of a Roman Camp at Wallhill.

Although nothing quite as ancient will be seen on this walk, the Tudor manor house of Little Moreton Hall and the lovely old church at Astbury will provide some interesting historical scenery.

Little Moreton Hall lies close to the A34 road 3 miles to the south-west of Congleton. Park the car in a lay-by which is at the side of the A34 road between the entrance to Little Moreton Hall and Cuttleford Farm. (Map ref. 831 589). Alternatively, you may wish to precede the walk with a visit to Little Moreton Hall, in which case you can leave the car on the large car park which is specifically for visitors. (There is a charge here which is refundable on visiting the hall.)

On leaving the car, follow the roadside pavement and pass Cuttleford Farm entrance drive. After 150 metres turn left and go through a field gate. Proceed with a hedge on the left at first, then walk forward across a field bearing slightly left and aiming to the left of a dwelling which can be seen straight ahead. Go through a hedge gap and continue with a ditch and hedge on your right. Go over a stile at the side of a gate and arrive at a crossing lane. Turn right and shortly pass the entrance drive of Alcumlow Hall Farm, then almost immediately keep left where the lane forks. The lane crosses a stream and leads to a junction.

Turn left and after 120 metres turn right and pass in front of a row of houses. Enter a facing grassy track between trees. Continue, then emerge onto a crossing lane. Cross this lane and bear left slightly, then forward, to follow a rough lane which skirts to the left of a green area which has dwellings on its far side. The lane quickly passes a house and leads towards a large farm. Do not continue towards the farmhouse, but turn right at the side of a barn, to continue along a winding grassy track between hedgerows.

Astbury Church now comes into view, and there are long views beyond to the hills of the Peak District National Park.

Keep forward along the hedged-in track and keep forward where a track goes off to the right. The track terminates at a field gate. Go over a stile here and continue along a facing field edge. Cross a double stile.

Over to the left, on a rise, is Bent Farm, but continue forward to cross a field, keeping a hedge on the right about 20 metres away. Cross a facing stile and turn right along a narrow lane. Shortly a crossing road is met where the way is right, then left, to arrive at the village of Astbury.

Although the village is very close to the busy A34 road and Congleton, it has retained much of its original character. During early spring the green in front of the delightful cottages here is a sea of yellow as hundreds of daffodils awake from their winter dormancy.

Walk up facing steps and enter the church confines. The lower part of the church tower is Norman, whilst the remainder of the structure was finally completed in 1490 after many earlier alterations. The interior of the church contains many relics from the 13th, 14th and 15th centuries.

Leave the church grounds on the north side passing by an old supported yew tree which is reputed to be over 1,000 years old. Descend some steps to enter a lane where the way is right. Pass the entrance drive of Glebe Farm and continue past School Lane and School House Farm. Keep right where the lanes fork and enter Dodds Lane. The lane takes you past Bank Farm and leads to a bridge which passes over the Macclesfield Canal. Leave the lane here and descend steps to arrive on the canal tow path. Turn right and pass under bridge 80.

Keep forward along the canal tow-path and pass under bridges 81, 82, 83, 84 and 85. Almost ½ mile after passing under bridge 85 another bridge is arrived at (not numbered). A sign here points towards Little Moreton Hall. Leave the canal side here and go over a stile to join the track which has come over the bridge. The track bears slightly left shortly and leads to a field gate. Go over a stile at the side of this gate and turn right to proceed along a field edge with a hedge on your right. Continue for two field lengths and cross two stiles. Bear diagonally left now, keeping in the direction of farm buildings ahead. Go over a stile and along a field edge, passing close to the farmhouse. Another stile takes you onto the entrance driveway of Little Moreton Hall.

The moated hall, which was the ancestral home of the Moreton family until acquired by the National Trust in 1937, has been little altered since it was built and is a fine example of 16th century half-timber work. Externally, the building has many carved gables and ornate windows, whilst internally there is impressive panelling, furniture and pewter.

A gentle stroll takes you back to either the visitors car park or the lay-by on the A34 road.

DANEBRIDGE

WALK 13

2½ miles (4 km)

OS map 118

Danebridge is at the border between Cheshire and Staffordshire. It lies midway between Macclesfield and Leek in the area bounded by the A54 and A523 roads.

Park at the side of the road on the Cheshire side of the bridge, taking care to allow enough room for access to and from the bridge. (Map ref. 965 652).

On leaving the car enter a track at Tolls Farm and continue past a trout pool which is on your right. On arriving at Pingle Cottage, enter a path on the left which commences over a small footbridge. Quickly pass

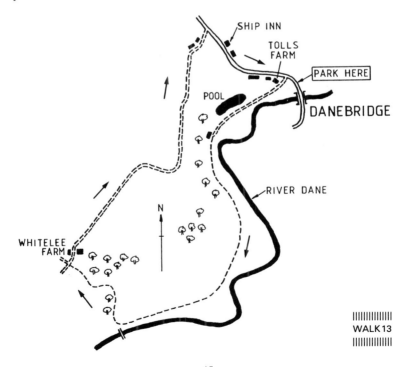

over two stiles and follow a path straight ahead which stays close to the river.

The river Dane is the main tributary of the river Weaver. It rises on Axe Edge and at first separates Cheshire from Staffordshire. It winds through Congleton and Holmes Chapel before entering the Weaver at Northwich.

The path continues along the lower level ground and eventually leads to a large metal footbridge which crosses the river Dane. Do not cross this bridge but turn sharp right to climb up the field edge, keeping close to a stream on your left. Cross a stile at the side of a stone gateway, cross the stream, and climb forward to immediately cross a second stile which takes you into a field. Bear right and climb up the field, keeping trees and a fence on your right, to go over a stile at the left of Whitelee Farm.

Looking back from here there are splendid views across to the Staffordshire Moors.

Go through the farmyard and walk forward along a lane which leads away from the farm. The lane, which passes through five gateways, dips and turns between trees for ¾ mile, and from it excellent views of the surrounding hills can be seen.

On meeting a crossing road turn right and descend past the Ship Inn. The ship depicted on the colourful signboard here is Nimrod, in which Sir Phillip Brocklehurst, a local landowner, accompanied the explorer Shackleton on one of his expeditions to the Antarctic.

A gentle descent takes you back to the car.

RIVER WEAVER

WALK 14

★

5½ miles (9 km)

OS map 117

The river Weaver is entirely in Cheshire. It rises close to the village of Peckforton, flows south at first towards Audlem, then turns north and passes through Nantwich, Winsford and Northwich to enter the Mersey close to Frodsham. The river has played an important part in the economic development of the county since 1763 when the Weaver Navigation from Winsford to Frodsham Bridge was completed, and part of this walk passes alongside this pleasant waterway.

One mile off the A56 road on the Warrington side of Frodsham lies the village of Aston. Park the car near the church of St Peter, taking care to leave access for other road users. (Map ref. 555 785).

Walk along the lane away from the church, pass the War Memorial and the stump of an old cross, to where the lane turns sharply to the left near a sign for Dutton. Enter a facing no-through-road here and walk past a lodge house and other dwellings. Pass a driveway on the right where a sign reads 'Private Road to Parkside Farm'. The lane takes you past a number of large detached houses and turns sharply to the right past a hedged-in track which goes off to the left. Follow the lane past a large farm called Aston Grange. The lane turns to the left and meets a facing gate close to farm outbuildings. Go through the gate, pass the outbuildings, then turn right through a gate to follow a track.

The track is a fine vantage point for long views across the surrounding countryside. The track turns right, descends, and turns left to a field gate. Go through this gate, turn right, and walk down to the river Weaver where the way is left along a riverside path.

Although the river has been used as a means of transport since medieval times, it was the discovery of rock salt near Winsford in 1670 which caused it to be considerably enlarged. The salt tax of the time ate into the profits of the carriers, but nevertheless, fairly large profits were accrued, these paying for, amongst other things, the repair of Chester Castle and the erection of Knutsford Jail. Although salt is still mined in the area, pleasure craft account for the majority of present day river traffic.

The riverside path takes you past a couple of dwellings then under the massive stone structure of Dutton railway viaduct. Continue for a short distance to a large footbridge which crosses an inlet of the river. Do not cross this bridge but turn left and keep forward along the left hand bank

47

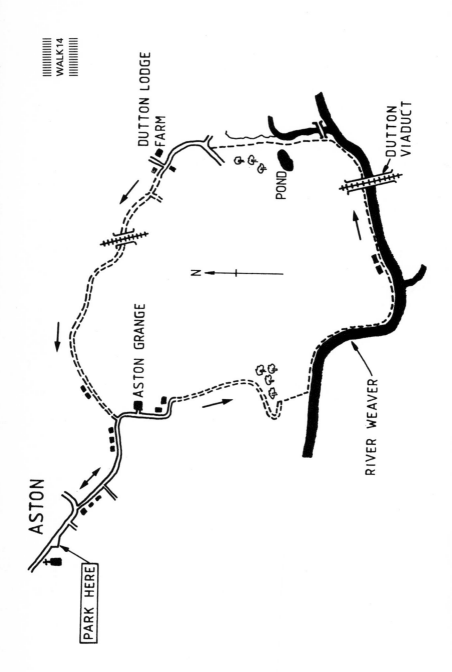

WALK14

ASTON

PARK HERE

DUTTON LODGE
FARM

DUTTON LODGE

N

ASTON GRANGE

POND

DUTTON
VIADUCT

RIVER WEAVER

of the inlet to cross a metal stile at the side of a large pond. The inlet turns away to the right now, but walk forward along level ground keeping a stream on your right and a high wooded bank on your left. Go over a stile in a crossing fence and follow the path across an undulating field. The path converges with a lane. Turn right, immediately pass a turn-off to the right, and climb towards Dutton Lodge Farm. Pass through a gate near outbuildings then immediately turn left between outbuildings to descend along a track. Keep forward past a turn-off to the left and go through a facing gate. Climb slightly, then pass through a tunnel under the railway. Walk forward now and climb along a facing track. Go over two stiles and walk along a hedged-in track which takes you past a couple of dwellings.

Emerge from the track and enter a lane. Turn right here and proceed back to Aston and the car.

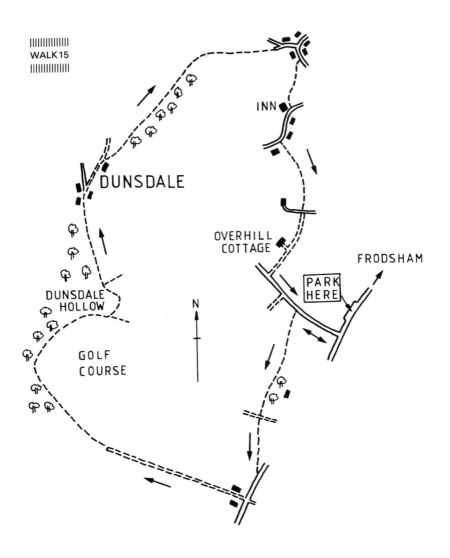

WALK 15

DUNSDALE

INN

OVERHILL
COTTAGE

FRODSHAM

PARK
HERE

DUNSDALE
HOLLOW

GOLF
COURSE

N

50

DUNSDALE

WALK 15

★

4 miles (6.5 km)

OS map 117

This walk traverses a high ridge which is at the rear of Frodsham and Helsby. It is a route which will appeal to the more adventurous, as it passes close to high cliffs where a head for heights and a good sense of direction are required.

Drive along Manley Road, which starts ¾ mile from the centre of Frodsham off the B5152 road. The road is headed by a sign which reads 'Mersey View 1 mile—Manley 3 miles'. The road climbs and winds, then levels out for a short distance. On the right hand side of the road there is a verge parking area just prior to a turnoff on the right where a sign indicates Forest Hills Hotel. (Map ref. 522 764).

On leaving the car, walk forward and turn right in the direction of the Forest Hills Hotel. Proceed for 200 metres then go over a stile on the left where a sign points to Manley Road. Walk along a field edge, cross a stile, and continue with a fence on the left and a hedge on the right. Keep forward past a path which goes to Manley Road and keep ahead in the direction of Manley. There are long views towards the Mersey estuary over to the right here.

Go over a farm approach track and enter a field over a tall stile. Bear slightly left as you walk across this field and go over a further stile to join a road. Turn right, then after 200 metres turn right again to proceed down a track headed by a sign which points to Woodhouse Hill. Go through a pair of facing gates and keep forward. Enter trees and descend. The path forks. Follow the right fork. You have now joined the Sandstone Trail, which you will follow for the next mile.

The trail is indicated by way markers—small wooden squares engraved with a footprint containing the letter S, together with a directional arrow. (See walks 24 to 30 inclusive.)

Climb through trees and follow the trail as it turns to the right. There is a large field over on your right here. On reaching more level ground the trail continues through a gully where there is a low overgrown stone wall on the right. Pass over the crest of the hill, descend, and bear right to follow a well defined path.

A rock slab on the left provides a vantage point for fine panoramic views. Over to the left is Helsby Hill, whilst straight ahead the sweeping waters of the Mersey estuary dominate the scene.

The path stays close to the edge of a high ridge. Coming up on the right is Frodsham Golf Course, which opened in 1990. Care is required now because the path drops down an outcrop of sandstone rock. To the left is a large tree-filled valley known as Dunsdale Hollow. The path skirts around the hollow and passes large sandstone cliffs. On the right shortly is a large buttress of sandstone rock known as Jacob's Ladder. Keep left here in the direction of Helsby. Shortly, a stone abutment is reached with steps leading away from it on the left. Keep forward here and continue with a wall on your left, to arrive at a junction of ways near a house called 'Dunsdale'. Straight ahead is a macadam lane, but fork right to walk along a track which takes you past a small electricity sub-station. You are no longer walking along the Sandstone Trail.

Continue past a row of houses on the right, then climb with a stone wall on the immediate left to where the track forks at the top of the rise. Take the right fork here and climb through trees. Emerge from the track and enter a facing cobbled lane which takes you between houses to a crossing road. Turn right and after 60 metres ascend steps on the right which take you up to the Belle Monte Inn.

Pass to the front of the inn then turn right to ascend along a lane. After 80 metres turn left to leave the lane just before a large detached bungalow is reached. A sign here points to Simons Lane and Beacon Hill. Proceed along a well worn path and cross a stile to enter a sloping field. Climb forward, with a fence on your left, then go over two stiles in quick succession and on through trees to pass over a crossing lane. Go through a facing gate and proceed along a grassy track. Pass Overhill Cottage, then turn left where the track meets a lane to continue in the direction of Manley. The lane takes you past the entrance drive of Frodsham Golf Club.

Turn left at the junction ahead and walk back to the car which is parked on the left.

KINGSLEY

WALK 16

★

6¼ miles (10 km)

OS map 117

This walk traverses some of the old lanes and bridleways of Cheshire which were in use long before the advent of the present day system of surfaced roads and motorways.

Between Frodsham and Delamere and adjacent to the B5152 road is a large lake called Hatch Mere. At the side of the lake is the Carriers Inn. Opposite the inn is the Hatchmere Picnic Area where there are generous parking facilities. Park the car here. (Map ref. 555 721).

On leaving the car park turn right, then right again to enter a track where a sign points to Norley Road and School Lane. After 150 metres the track turns to the left, but keep forward here in the direction of School Lane. The path takes you onto a gravel track. Keep forward, pass a turning to the left, and arrive at a crossroads near a bungalow called Min-y-Coed. Turn left along School Lane, walk past Crabmill Lane and continue past Norley Church Sunday School, to arrive at another crossroads.

Down the lane to the left the square sandstone tower of Norley parish church can be seen, but the way is right, then immediately left, to enter Town Farm Lane, where a sign points to Crowton. After 400 metres the lane turns to the right and takes you past Town Farm. Turn next left to shortly pass a dwelling on the left called Westwood. The lane gradually descends and, after almost a mile, leads to a T-junction. Turn left along Kingsley Road in the direction of Frodsham and after ½ a mile turn left again to enter Roddy Lane. After 400 metres bear left where the lane forks. The lane takes you along level terrain at first and then climbs past Beech Cottage. Just before the top of the hill is reached, turn right through a field gate where a footpath sign points to Kingsley. Proceed down a short narrow track, which is enclosed by tall hedgerows. Emerge from the hedgerows and turn left to cross a stone stile. Turn right, and descend for one field's length keeping a hedge on your immediate right. Go over a stile at the side of some holly bushes then bear left and walk to a stile in a crossing hedgerow. Turn left and continue, keeping the hedgerow on your immediate left. At the field corner go over a stile to enter a hedged-in track. Turn right and follow this winding track until a crossing lane is met, close to dwellings. Turn left and enter the village of Kingsley.

Keep forward past Well Lane, pass the Hurst Methodist Church and

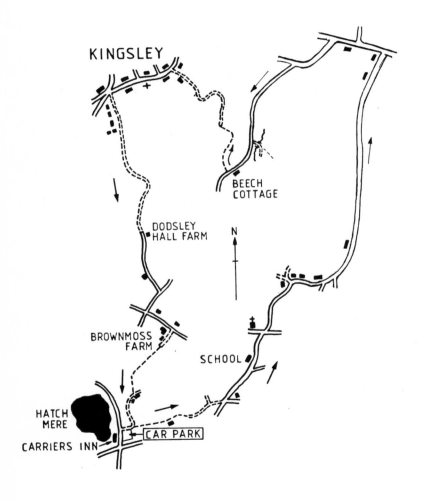

KINGSLEY

BEECH
COTTAGE

DODSLEY
HALL FARM

N

BROWNMOSS
FARM

SCHOOL

HATCH
MERE

CAR PARK

CARRIERS INN

54

a lane on the right, to arrive at a junction at Top Road. Turn left here to enter a bridleway, which is hemmed in at first by earth banks topped with trees and hedgerows. On reaching more level ground, the track is fenced in on both sides. Shortly, the track descends, then turns right to continue with a fence on the right and a hedge on the left. The way turns right and left and is now skirted by hedgerows. Emerge from the track to the side of Dodsley Hall Farm and continue forward along a macadam lane. Pass close to a second farm, then turn right at the junction ahead. Shortly crossroads are met where the way is left. Continue for 300 metres to arrive at Brownmoss Farm, which is on the right. Pass the farm and turn immediately right down a concrete drive where a sign points towards Hatchmere and School Lane. Pass close to the farm outbuildings, then go over a stile at the side of a gate. Follow a track as it bears to the left—there is a fence on the left here and a hedgerow on the right. Keep forward and walk along two field edges via a couple of stiles. Pass through a gate at the side of a dwelling and bear right in the direction of Hatchmere.

Follow a track. After 200 metres the track turns right and takes you back to Hatchmere, and the car.

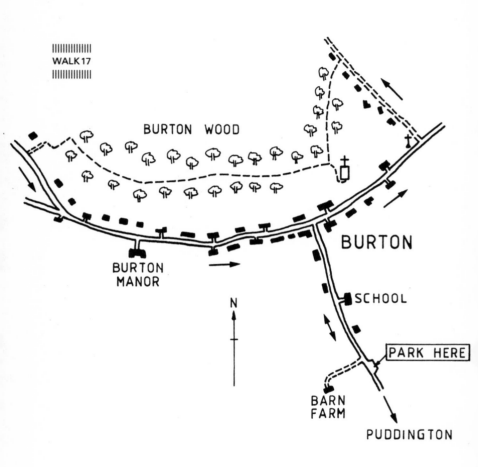

WALK 17

BURTON WOOD

BURTON

BURTON MANOR

N

SCHOOL

PARK HERE

BARN FARM

PUDDINGTON

BURTON

WALK 17

★

2 miles (3 km)

OS map 117

This short walk keeps within the precincts of the lovely Wirral village of Burton, a village full of interesting old houses and delightful picturesque cottages.

Burton lies close to the A540 road and is 8 miles north-west of Chester.

Drive down Puddington Lane away from the centre of the village, pass a school and arrive at a small parking area at the left hand side of the lane. Leave the car here. (Map ref. 320 739).

On leaving the car, walk back up Puddington Lane to the village centre. Turn right, pass the church entrance and the village hall, then turn next left to enter a track.

There is a stone cross on the left here. At the base of this cross there is a carved inscription relating to walkers!

Walk past large detached houses and turn left after 200 metres to go through a kissing gate close to Haddon Lodge. Continue along a narrow path. The path descends through trees, and leads down facing steps to Burton Church.

The church has many interesting features. Study the clock-face on the main tower and see if you can decide what the time is without checking your wristwatch. Firstly, there is only one hand. Secondly, the hours are split into four divisions, not five as with a conventional time-piece. Each division represents fifteen minutes. For example, if the hand points to one division past three, the time is a quarter past three etc. The clock was installed in 1751 and there are only five of a similar type in Great Britain. The church, which has a Jacobean altar rail, contains Saxon relics found during excavations on the site. The church is dedicated to Saint Nicholas, the Patron Saint of Mariners. This may seem odd, but at one time the village lay very close to the sea. The ensuing silting of the Dee estuary has pushed the sea farther away, leaving a dangerous marshland to the west of the former shoreline.

Leave the church up the same steps by which you arrived, then turn left to continue along level ground through trees. Shortly, a Quaker burial ground is reached, which dates from 1663.

The Quakers are buried in this lonely spot as they were not permitted church burial because of the prevailing religious conflicts of the 17th century.

The path continues and passes through a gap in a crossing fence. There are steps down on the left now, but keep forward in the same direction as before to follow a well-trodden path through Burton Wood. The path goes past the corner of a fence and leads to a stone stile not far from a kissing gate. Do not go over the stone stile but turn left and descend through the trees. The path turns right and left to enter a gully which leads to a kissing gate. Go through this gate and enter a road. Cross the road and turn left to follow a tree-lined pavement. There are long views to the right here across the low-lying silted marshes of the Dee estuary.

Descend some steps and keep left to follow the road into Burton village. Shortly, the gates of Burton Manor are reached on the right. Opposite is a delightful old thatched cottage. Keep forward past interesting houses and cottages, many of which are built directly onto outcrops of solid sandstone rock.

Continue, then turn next right to enter Puddington Lane which leads back to the car.

ASHTON

WALK 18

★

5 miles (8 km)

OS map 117

Centred on the village of Ashton, this walk combines easy-to-follow field paths and quiet country lanes, resulting in a pleasant and varied excursion into the Cheshire countryside.

The B5393 road joins the A54 road mid-way between Kelsall and Tarvin. One mile to the north of this junction is the village of Ashton. On the northern side of the village, and by the side of the B5393 road, there is a long roadside verge at the bottom of a hill between Mouldsworth Railway Station and Ashton Church. This parking area is between Delamare Road and Grange Road. (Map ref. 511 703).

Leave the car, walk forward, and turn left to enter Grange Road. Follow this pleasant 'lane' (it's far too narrow to be described as a road) for almost a mile, passing Ashton Grange and other dwellings, to arrive at a junction. Keep right here and gradually climb to pass Woodside Farm. Keep right at the next junction, but after a further 50 metres go over a stile in a hedgerow on the right where a sign indicates Kelsall. Turn left, and immediately cross a second stile. The way is right here, to continue with outbuildings and a fence on your right. After 60 metres go over a stile in the fence on the right, then quickly pass over a second stile to enter a large field. Bear diagonally left here, and walk forward keeping to the right of the first telegraph pole. Pass over a stile at the side of a large tree and go through a gap in a conifer hedge to enter a large field. This field is surrounded by tall hedges of conifers. Turn left and walk forward keeping the hedge you have just come through on your immediate left. Turn right at the field corner and continue with a hedge still on your left. At the field corner turn left and enter another field to gradually climb with a hedge still on your left. At the field corner the hedge on your left terminates. Turn right now and walk along the top edge of the field to continue past the end of a hedge on the right. The path bears gradually left now and enters a lane through a gap in a stone wall.

Turn right, and follow the lane for ¼ mile passing a lodge house and a dwelling called Warwick House. Turn next right to enter a hedged-in track which is headed by a sign which says 'Unsuitable for motors'. The track descends and offers long views towards Chester and beyond. Follow the track for a mile and enter the suburbs of the village of Ashton. Walk forward and pass Willowhayes, Pentre Close and Dunn's

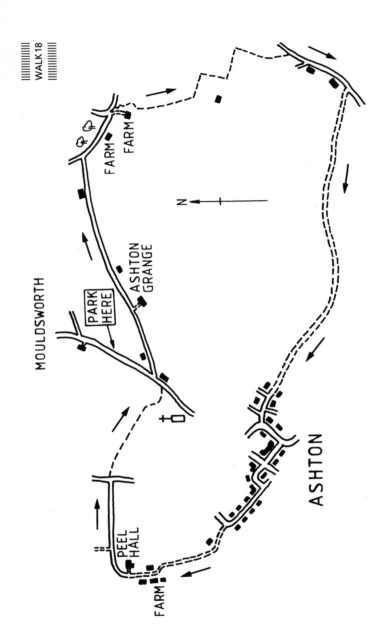

WALK 18

MOULDSWORTH

FARM
FARM

N

ASHTON
GRANGE

PARK
HERE

ASHTON

PEEL
HALL

FARM

Lane, then turn left along Duck Lane. Turn next right and keep forward past Vicar's Close to arrive at the Golden Lion Inn. Cross Church Road and enter West End. On passing West End Cottage the lane turns left and takes you to crossroads. Turn right here and follow the roadside footpath along a straight stretch of urban road. After 200 metres the road turns sharp right, but keep forward here between hedges. Pass the Scout Hut and go through a facing gate. Climb forward with a hedge on the left and after 70 metres go through another gate.

Straight ahead there is a farm. Walk forward keeping a fence on the right and then bear left to go through a gate on the right. Pass between farm outbuildings. The way is cobbled for a short distance and then a macadam drive takes you past the front of Peel Hall. Keep forward through a facing gate and follow the drive as it turns to the right. Ashton Church comes into view. The drive takes you to a crossing lane where the way is forward to go over a facing stile. Quickly cross a second stile and continue with a hedge on the left. Go over another stile then arrive at a kissing gate. Go through this gate and proceed with a hedge now on the right. Follow the hedge as it turns to the right and then go over a stile to enter a road.

Turn left and walk back to the car which is parked a short distance away.

LITTLE BUDWORTH

WALK 19

★

2¾ miles (4.5 km)

OS map 117

This walk commences close to the famous racing circuit of Oulton Park. The circuit is situated some 3 miles north-east of Tarporley, and lies close to the junction of the A49 and A54 roads. On summer Saturdays some traffic build-up in the area can be expected, due to the racing activity.

Leave the car at the Little Budworth Country Park car park, which is situated off Coach Road, a short distance from the main entrance to Oulton Park. (Map ref. 590 655).

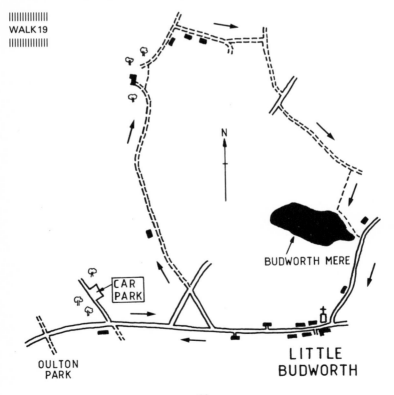

On leaving the car park turn left to walk along Coach Road. At the junction ahead can be seen a large stone arch which has three arrows mounted above it and a lodge on each side. On the other side of the arch is Lodge Corner, a well known bend on the racing circuit.

Turn left, then shortly turn left again to enter Park Road. Immediately after passing Pinfold Lane turn left again to follow a track between tree-lined verges. The track takes you past a dwelling and leads towards a large house. Keep to the right here and follow a path which descends and passes over a stream. The path bears right now and takes you up a tree-lined gully which leads onto a crossing track. Turn right here and continue past houses on the right, then turn right again to proceed down a lane which passes Hollybush Cottage and Hollybush Bungalow. The lane turns sharp right shortly, but the way is left to enter a grassy track. After 200 metres there is a junction of tracks. Turn right here and continue to a crossing lane. Turn right and left to keep forward along a further track.

Shortly, a typical Cheshire scene comes into view straight ahead. In the foreground is Budworth Mere, whilst on a rise to its rear is the village of Little Budworth, with its church dominant.

The track descends and a stile is reached on the right where a sign points towards Budworth Mere. Cross this stile and walk straight down to the edge of Budworth Mere, crossing a further two stiles en route. At the water's edge turn left and continue along a waterside path to a facing stile. Cross the stile, then turn right along a lane, to arrive at the village of Little Budworth.

During the reign of Charles I, Little Budworth sported a famous horse track and many well supported meetings were held. Sadly, this track has long since disappeared, together with the old church which was replaced by a rather plain building in 1800.

. Follow the lane between the Red Lion Inn and the church, to shortly pass Booth Avenue and the War Memorial. Keep forward now, to arrive back at Coach Road and the car park.

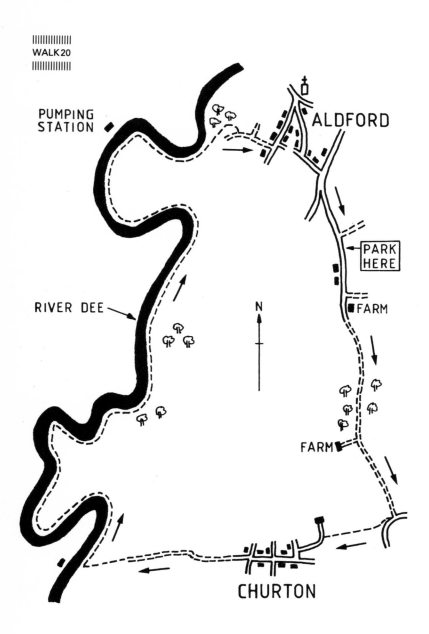

WALK 20

PUMPING
STATION

ALDFORD

PARK
HERE

RIVER DEE

N

FARM

FARM

CHURTON

ALDFORD

★

7 miles (11 km)

OS map 117

This is the longest walk in the book, but the route stays on level ground and is easy going, passing through the interesting border villages of Churton and Aldford, which are connected by a scenic riverside path.

Driving south through Aldford on the B5130 road, pass the Grosvenor Arms Hotel then Rushmere Lane on the right, to turn down the next lane on the left, which is a no-through-road. After 200 metres pass a track which goes off to the left and park the car on the left, where there is good verge parking available. (Map ref. 422 586).

Leave the car and proceed down the lane, passing cottages on the right then a track and a farm on the left. Go through a facing gate and continue along a well-defined track. Keep forward along this track for 1 mile, keeping forward where there is a turn-off to the right which leads to a farm. The track emerges at a bend in a crossing lane. Go through a gate on the right here and walk across a narrow field to quickly go over a stile and footbridge. The path continues between a hedge and fence. Cross another stile and walk forward along a macadam drive straight ahead. Arrive at a cattle grid where you have a choice of gate or stile. Continue, turn left at a crossing lane, then next right by Churton Hall, a fine old black and white building now used as a farm. Shortly crossroads are met where the way is forward down Hob Lane, passing to the left of the White Horse Hotel. Keep on past Churton Methodist Church then go forward to enter a facing hedged-in track.

The track gradually descends, and winds, then continues with a long holly hedge on the right. Go through a facing gate and proceed in the direction of buildings which come into view straight ahead. On getting closer to these buildings it can be seen that they are on the far bank of the river Dee and are, in fact, in Wales.

On reaching the river bank turn right and shortly pass over stiles in front of a small bungalow. Continue, and then go over a stile in a crossing fence.

Keep forward along the riverside for almost 3 miles, passing over a number of stiles en route.

The river Dee rises in the Welsh hills, then feeds a large lake at Bala before flowing through Llangollen, Farndon and Chester to its estuary and the open sea. Pleasure craft account for the majority of present day river traffic, but in much earlier times the river was a well utilised means of transport. This stretch of river was certainly navigable during the medieval period, for there are records of goods being sent along it between Overton and Chester.

Caution has to be exercised in order not to miss the point where the path leaves the riverside. The guiding point is a large red brick building on the opposite bank. This building is in fact a Pumping Station. Shortly after passing this building the river turns to the right and leads to a small riverside wood. Cross a stile here and enter the wood. Follow a path between the trees. The path turns right and leads to a track where the way is left. Follow the track as it bears right, and gradually climb to arrive at a large gate and a small one set across the track. Go through the small gate then turn left where the track meets a lane. Straight ahead Aldford Parish Church can be seen. Walk up to the church passing quaint old houses and cottages. Turn right, then go down Middle Lane, which commences opposite the church entrance. Pass the post office, followed by houses painted in a picturesque fashion similar to those often seen in some continental villages.

Turn next left, and then right, to shortly arrive at the lane down which the car is parked.

BUNBURY

WALK 21

★

3¼ miles (5.25 km)

OS map 117

The ancient village of Bunbury lies in rich farming country close to the Central Cheshire Sandstone Ridge. The village, which is dominated by a very beautiful church, has a long history and is mentioned in the Domesday Book. Although many of its old half timbered cottages have long since disappeared, the village has much to offer the discerning eye.

The walk commences at Haughton Moss, a tiny village which is 2 miles east of Spurstow and the A49 road.

At the centre of the village there is a junction of lanes, one of which leads to Haughton Hall. To the left of this lane there is a no-through-road. Leave the car at the right hand side of this road where there is good verge parking. (Map ref. 577 564).

On leaving the car, walk down the no-through-road. The road leads onto a track and takes you to a stile at the side of a facing field gate shortly after passing a small farm. Cross the stile and enter a long narrow field. Bear slightly right and continue, to cross a small footbridge which takes you over a stream. Quickly cross a stile in a facing hedgerow and climb forward into a large field. At the top of the rise bear slightly left and walk to a stile in a facing hedgerow. Cross the stile. There is a track on the right here but walk forward keeping a hedge on your immediate right. Shortly, a facing field gap is met with a small wooden gate at its left hand side. Go through this gate and keep forward through two further gates to where the path is hedged-in on both sides. Continue along this path for 100 metres, then cross a stile in the right hand hedge at the side of a tree. Continue along a field edge keeping a hedgerow on your right and pass over two fences followed by a stile. Walk forward now, keeping in the same general direction as before, and go over another stile at the field corner which is situated close by some bungalows. Pass between the bungalows and emerge onto a road near to the Methodist church. Turn right and enter the village of Bunbury.

Keep right along Bunbury Lane, pass the Nags Head Hotel and Wyche Lane, and enter Vicarage Lane. Pass the Vicarage, descend, then climb up to Bunbury parish church, sited on a rise straight ahead.

The church is dedicated to St Boniface, who became the Apostle of Germany and died in 755. The church contains the alabaster tomb and effigy of Sir Hugh Calveley, a distinguished soldier who died in 1394. The roof was extensively damaged in 1940 when a landmine fell onto

67

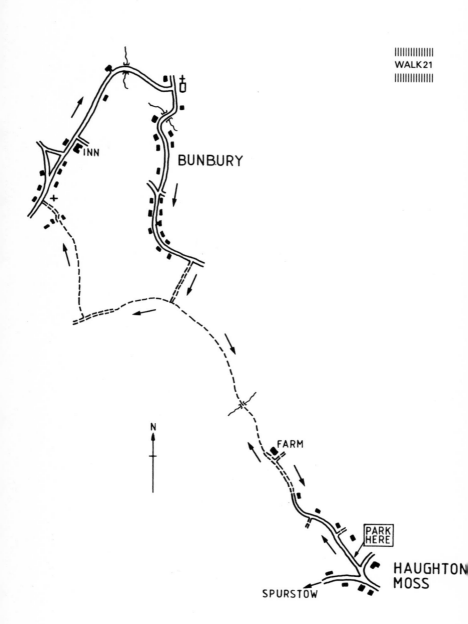

BUNBURY

INN

N

FARM

PARK
HERE

HAUGHTON
MOSS

SPURSTOW

68

Higher Bunbury. Thankfully, the main structure of the church remained intact and all the damaged areas have now been restored.

From the church, descend along Wyche Road. The lane winds past old cottages and crosses the infant river Gowy. Continue to a junction of lanes. Turn left here along Wyche Lane and follow the lane as it turns to the left near a house called 'Ericeira'. Continue along the lane for a further 80 metres, then turn right to enter a track at the side of a field gate. A sign here says 'Public Footpath—Haughton'. The track leads into a large field. Do not enter this field but cross a stile on your left.

You are now back on part of the original route. Walk forward and pass over stile and footbridge to eventually join the lane which leads back to the car.

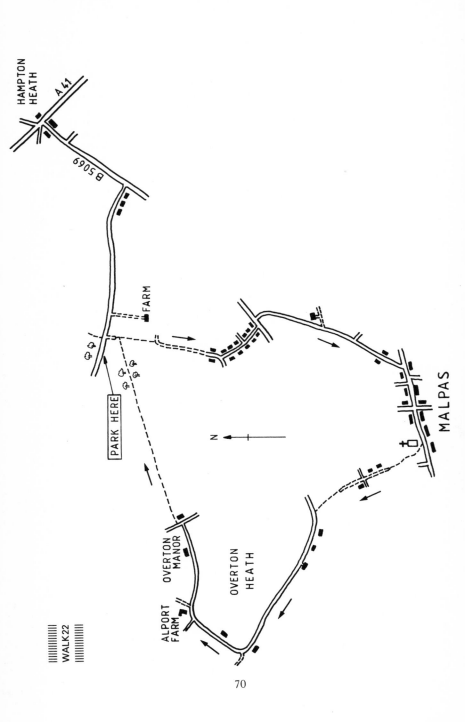

HAMPTON HEATH

A 41

B 5069

FARM

PARK HERE

N

MALPAS

OVERTON MANOR

ALPORT FARM

OVERTON HEATH

WALK 22

70

MALPAS

4 miles (6.5 km)

OS map 117

Situated in south-west Cheshire close to the Welsh border, Malpas has played an important role in the history of the county. The Romans had an encampment here and the Normans built a castle. Although only traces of these early settlements remain, the present-day town contains many interesting buildings and is dominated by a magnificent 14th century church.

The B5069 road connects Malpas with the A41 road at Hampton Heath. Between these two places, ½ mile from Hampton Heath and 1¼ miles from Malpas, there is a secondary road which joins the B5069 road. It is the only through road on the westerly side of the B5069 road between these two places. A road sign at the head of this secondary road reads 'Tilston 3 & Farndon 7'. Drive down this secondary road for ½ mile to where, on the left, there is good verge parking available. This parking place is about 250 metres past a farm entrance drive on the left and 80 metres past the point where a footpath crosses the road. (Map ref. 489 488).

On leaving the car, walk back along the road for 80 metres and turn right to enter a short length of track which, after 30 metres, leads to a field gate. Go over a stile at the side of this gate and climb forward along a path which follows a field edge. Cross a stile at the field corner and proceed along a facing hedged-in track. Emerge from the track at a stile and walk forward along a road which takes you between bungalows. Bear next left along Hollowood Road and keep forward past Hebers Close. Cross the main road, bearing left, and enter Greenway Lane. Follow this narrow sunken lane for ½ mile, keeping right at two junctions, to arrive at a crossing road. Turn right here and keep forward to gently climb in the direction of the church. Pass Leech Road and Well Avenue then go over a crossing road and ascend steps between the Crown Hotel and the Thurlow Memorial. This is the centre of Malpas. Keep forward where the road passes between quaint old shops and enter the church confines through a wrought iron gateway.

Standing on the site of an earlier church, the present church was built during the 14th century and then re-modelled a hundred years later in keeping with the developments in architecture which were taking place at that time. The church is dedicated to Oswald, King of Northumbria, who was killed in battle during the year 642. If time permits, take a look inside this architectural gem.

Enter the church by the south porch, over which there is an old sundial. The church contains many items of interest. On entering, a magnificent 13th century iron-clad chest can be seen. The nave ceiling has been painstakingly restored to good effect. Of major interest are the Brereton and Cholmondeley chapels, which contain superb medieval monuments dedicated to earlier members of these well known Cheshire families.

A detailed illustrated brochure describing points of interest for visitors is available inside the church.

On leaving the south porch, bear right, and make for a gateway which has a lamp mounted above it. Fork right up three steps 12 metres before the gateway is reached and continue along a grassy path. On the right there is a high mound, this being all that remains of the old castle. Over a wall on the right in a short distance there is a bowling green. The path becomes hedged-in and takes you past a second bowling green. Keep forward across a macadam drive and enter a narrow path through a facing gate at the right hand side of a bungalow called Tall Trees. Climb slightly. Go over a stile and cross a facing field to arrive at a kissing gate.

There are long views over to the left here and if the day is clear the Welsh hills should be visible.

Go through the kissing gate. Descend steps to enter a lane. Turn left and follow the lane as it descends to the scattered hamlet of Overton Heath. Continue, passing isolated dwellings, and follow the lane as it turns to the right and gradually climbs. Follow the lane as it turns to the right again close to the entrance drive of Overton Hall and Alport Farm, and continue to shortly pass Overton Manor. Arrive at a T junction opposite a dwelling. Turn left and then immediately right to go over a stile at the side of a field gate.

Keeping a hedge on your immediate right follow the edge of three fields and cross three stiles. On crossing the third stile there are a couple of small footbridges to negotiate. A further stile gives access to a tree-lined path. Walk forward between the trees. Emerge from the path and go over a stile on the left, which is at the side of a field gate. Walk forward to a crossing road.

Turn left now and walk back to the car which is parked 80 metres away on the left.

MARBURY

WALK 23

★

3 miles (5 km)

OS map 117

The tiny picturesque village of Marbury-cum-Quoisley is tucked away in a quiet green corner of Cheshire, 3 miles to the north of Whitchurch. The village lies between two meres and its lovely old church rests on a gentle hillside overlooking the larger mere.

From the centre of Marbury village drive in the direction of Bickley. Pass the church entrance. Shortly a junction of lanes is met. Follow the lane to the left which is signed to Wirswall and Malpas. At the next junction bear left again, this time in the direction of Wirswall. After a further 350 metres there is good verge parking available on the left hand side, close to where a footpath sign points across the fields. (Map ref. 555 460).

Cross the stile and walk forward, bearing slightly left, to go over a stile at the field corner. Continue, with a fence and narrow ditch on your immediate right then go over a stream via an old overgrown footbridge. Walk forward, in the direction of Marbury church which comes into view straight ahead, but after 30 metres bear left to go over a stile at the left hand side of a field gate. Proceed, aiming to the left of a row of single-storey dwellings to enter a lane over a stile. Turn right and walk towards Marbury village centre, then turn right again to shortly enter the church confines through a lych gate.

Records show that a church existed at Marbury in 1299. The present church of St Michael's dates from the 15th century and its outward appearance resembles that of St Oswald's, Malpas, although the latter is much larger. The original and extremely well preserved 15th century pulpit is still in use.

Leave the church grounds through a small gate close to an old gnarled tree. Keep forward with a fence on your left and go over a stile to enter a lane. Turn left, and then next right, to pass in front of the Swan Inn. Continue for ¼ mile and then go over a stile on the right, some 30 metres after passing a dwelling on the left. Follow a field edge, keeping a hedgerow on your immediate right. The path follows the hedgerow as it bends to the right and takes you towards a small farm which can be seen straight ahead. Cross two stiles in quick succession and pass between the farmhouse and outbuildings to enter a facing grassy track via a stile.

73

||||||||||||||||
WALK 23
||||||||||||||||

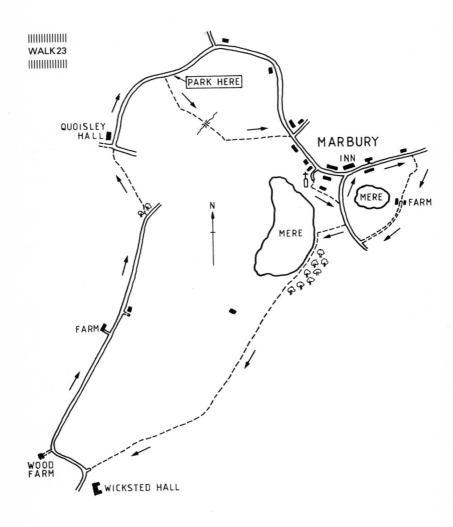

PARK HERE

QUOISLEY
HALL

MARBURY

INN

N

MERE

MERE

FARM

FARM

WOOD
FARM

WICKSTED HALL

Over to the right, through trees, can be seen the still waters of the small mere.

A stile in a crossing hedgerow to the right of a gate takes you onto a lane. Turn right and continue, but after 120 metres go through a field gate on the left. A footpath sign here indicates Wirswall. Keep forward and walk down to the edge of the large mere. Turn left and continue along the water's edge to arrive at a gate.

Looking back from here there is a delightful view of the church.

Go through the gate. Keep forward along the water's edge. There are trees on the left here. Pass through another gate and enter a large field. Keep forward here, with trees still on the left. A facing gate is shortly met close to where a solitary house sits on top of a rise on the right. Go through this gate and walk forward along a grassy hollow, then climb to go over a stile which is at the side of a further field gate. Climb forward, and bear left, to cross a stile by a small gate.

From here Wicksted Hall can be seen sited on high ground straight ahead. Climb the facing hill, aiming to the right of the hall. Two thirds of the way up the hill go over a stile at the side of a field gate. Continue with a hawthorn hedge on your immediate left. A stile takes you onto a lane. Turn right and pass Wood Farm. Follow the lane as it descends past a farm and a dwelling on the right called Deemster House. The lane levels out and gently turns to the right. Follow a footpath on the left here which commences through a thicket. Enter a field and continue along the field edge keeping a fence on your left. Go over a crossing fence. Walk forward along level ground for 100 metres then climb to the right to pass over a stile in a hedge. Walk forward down a facing lane and quickly pass a farm on the left called Quoisley Hall.

Follow the lane for a further 400 metres to arrive back at the car, which is parked on the right.

WALK 24

HATCH MERE

CARRIERS INN

CAR PARK

EDDISBURY LODGE

FARM

N

INN

FARM

PRIMROSE HILL

PRIMROSE HILL

WALK 24

★

5½ miles (9 km)

OS map 117

The solitude of the forest paths, coupled with long views across the surrounding countryside, combine to make this walk a memorable one.

The bulk of Delamere Forest is situated between the B5152 and B5393 roads. Running through the forest between Mouldsworth and Hatchmere is a road generally known as the 'switchback road', because of its undulating surface. Drive along this road to where, about one mile from Hatchmere a sign indicates Barns Bridge Gates—Sandstone Trail. Here there is a picnic area and car park which is set in a banked clearing in the forest. (Map ref. 542 715).

Leave the car here and climb some steps up the banking on the right. On top of the banking a sign indicates Beeston Castle—this is the start of the Sandstone Trail.

Follow the trail through the forest, keeping an eye open for the way markers—small wooden squares engraved with a footprint containing the letter S, together with a directional arrow. Follow the trail over the railway and then cross a stile. Keep forward and then emerge from the forest at another stile close by Eddisbury Lodge. Turn left, and then right, towards Beeston Castle. Climb along a gravel track and pass a small farm. The track becomes grassy and leads to a stile at the side of a facing gate.

Looking back from here there are extensive views over Delamere Forest and the surrounding countryside.

Continue forward and descend to a crossing road. Cross the road, turn left, and walk across a small car park to go over a stile where a sign indicates Beeston Castle. Descend a long staircase of wooden steps between trees. Follow the path as it winds and climbs through trees. Go through a gap in a crossing fence and continue, to pass over a stile. Follow a well-defined path and climb through trees. This is Primrose Hill.

The path reaches level ground and leads to a junction of paths. The Sandstone Trail turns to the left and descends, but bear right here and leave the trail to follow a path where, after 40 metres, there is a field over the hedgerow on your right. Continue, descending slightly, to a crossing track. Turn right and follow the track in the direction of King's Gate. The track climbs to meet a lane, where the way is right. Pass The Sandstone House on the left, then Delamere Farm on the right. Follow the lane as it turns sharp right, then keep forward for ½ mile and descend to a crossing road. On the left is Th'Ouse at Top Inn, whilst straight ahead is Yeld Lane, where a sign says 'Mouldsworth 3 miles'.

Enter Yeld Lane. Keep forward for a mile, climbing at first, then descend to where the lane turns sharp left. Leave the lane to the right here and follow a track between tall hedgerows to arrive at a facing gate. Go through a gap at the side of the gate and walk forward along the facing track to where a sign on the left indicates Barns Bridge Gates. You are now back on the Sandstone Trail.

Retrace your initial steps, cross the railway, and follow the Sandstone Trail back to the car park.

WILLINGTON CORNER

WALK 25

★

6¼ miles (10 km)

OS map 117

This walk will take you along undulating country paths through the very heart of central Cheshire, where there are fine views across miles of rolling, wooded countryside.

On the western side of Kelsall, close to where the A54 by-pass road begins, there is an inn called Th'Ouse at Top. Drive along Waste Lane, which begins at the side of the inn. The lane is straight and climbs for almost ½ mile, then turns sharp left. A quarter of a mile further on there is a small car park on the left where a Forestry Commission sign indicates Primrose Wood. (Map ref. 535 678).

Leave the car and go through a gateway at the side of the parking area to descend along a track which leads into Delamere Forest. After ¼ mile the track bends to the right and joins the Sandstone Trail. After a further 60 metres the trail leaves the track and follows a path which goes off to the right.

Be careful not to miss the turn off to the right, which is indicated by a way marker—a small wooden square engraved with a footprint containing the letter S, together with a directional arrow.

The path proceeds through dense forest at first, then turns left and climbs to a stile on the right. Cross the stile and climb forward up a facing field, keeping a hedge on the immediate right. Go through a kissing gate, then proceed along level ground with a hedge now on the left. A stile gives access to a narrow hedged-in path. Cross another stile and walk forward to arrive at a lane. Keep forward along the lane for 50 metres, passing a pond on the right, then turn right to enter a narrow banked-in path where a sign indicates Fishers Green and Tarporley. The path gradually descends.

Straight ahead is the Cheshire Plain, and if the day is clear you should be able to see the Welsh hills in the distance.

After ¾ mile, the path emerges at a crossing lane. Turn left here and proceed along the lane for 250 metres, then cross a stile on the right. Continue with a hedge on the right to cross a second stile.

From here, Beeston Castle can be seen sitting on an outcrop of rock 4 miles away, straight ahead.

Turn left and continue along a field edge with a hedge on the left. Go over a stile in a crossing hedge then turn right to proceed down a hedged-in cow-lane. Continue forward over two further stiles, then walk

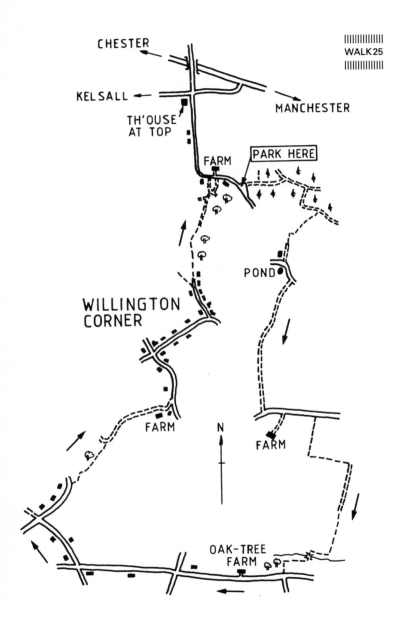

CHESTER

WALK 25

KELSALL

MANCHESTER

TH'OUSE
AT TOP

FARM

PARK HERE

POND

WILLINGTON
CORNER

FARM

N

FARM

OAK-TREE
FARM

80

forward along a field edge keeping a hedge on your left. Turn right at the field corner to proceed with a stream and hedge on the immediate left. The trail crosses the stream via a footbridge and continues with a fence and the stream now on the right. Turn left at a facing hedge and then go over a stile which leads into a lane.

Leave the Sandstone Trail here and turn right to follow the lane. Pass Oak-Tree Farm and keep straight ahead at the crossroads. Continue for almost ½ mile to the next crossroads, where the way is right. Pass Pembroke House, then arrive at a T junction where the way is right. The lane continues past Holly Bank and Ivy Cottage and turns sharp left, but keep forward here to enter a grassy track between hedgerows. Pass through a gate and continue to a second facing gate. Do not go through this facing gate but go through a gate on the immediate right. Bear left and proceed with a hedge on the left at first then, after 50 metres, bear right to a crossing fence at the side of a tall ash tree. This fence is 25 metres past a telegraph pole. Cross the fence and enter a large field. Keep forward along the left hand side of the field, then walk forward along a concrete track which follows the field edge. The track leads towards a farm. Pass through two gates close to the farm outbuildings, then follow a track which turns to the left away from the farmhouse to meet a crossing lane. Keep left and follow the lane for ¼ mile, to arrive at a crossroads.

This is Willington Corner. Turn right along Chapel Lane. Pass the Methodist Chapel (now a private dwelling), then fork left to enter Gooseberry Lane. The lane climbs past a mixture of old and new dwellings and gives access to a narrow path which climbs up the facing hill. The path drops away to the left here, so take care.

Pause before reaching the hilltop and turn to admire the fine view across the Cheshire Plain.

Cross a stile at the top of the climb. Bear right and after 150 metres go over a stile at the side of a metal gate. Continue along a facing track with a fence on the immediate right. Cross two further stiles, then continue with a hedge on the left and cross a gravel track to arrive at a crossing lane.

Turn right by the post box and keep on past Delamere Farm to shortly arrive back at the car, which is parked on the left.

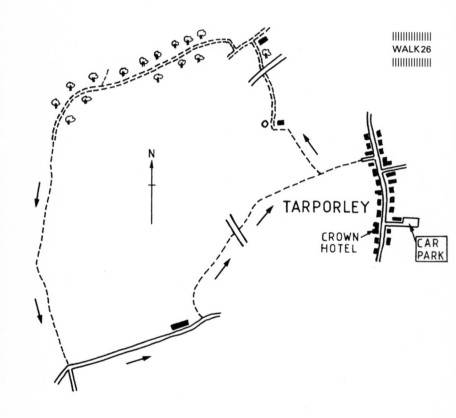

WALK 26

TARPORLEY

CROWN HOTEL

CAR PARK

N

TARPORLEY

WALK 26

★

3½ miles (5.5 km)

OS map 117

Many years ago, long before McAdam had invented his system of road-making, the lanes of Cheshire were mostly hedged-in tracks. This walk will enable you to sample some of these tracks and will give an idea of what travel must have been like prior to the Industrial Revolution.

The walk commences at the elegant Georgian town of Tarporley, which lies on the A49 road 10 miles to the west of Chester.

Opposite the Crown Hotel in the centre of Tarporley is the entrance to a free car park at the rear of the British Legion Club. (Map ref. 555 624).

On leaving the car park turn right along Tarporley High Steet. Pass Park Road and the Police Station, then turn left to arrive at the lych gate entrance of St Helen's Church.

St Helen, although not a Saint of the Gospel, was the mother of the Roman Emperor Constantine, who is generally accepted as being the first Christian Emperor. A church has stood on this site for many centuries, but the present building was completed in 1878 and is in the Gothic style.

Go through a gate on the left, where a sign indicates Birch Heath. The footpath skirts the edge of the churchyard and leads to a kissing gate. Pass through this gate and enter a field. Keep forward for 30 metres and then bear right to walk in the direction of a house, half hidden by trees some 400 metres away. The path approximately follows a line of telegraph poles across the field and there is also a fence on the left. On nearing the house, go over a stile in the fence on the left and walk forward keeping a hedge on your immediate right. After 50 metres cross a stile on the right at the side of a gate. Pass between a pond and the front of the house to enter a hedged-in track. The track leads to the Tarporley By-pass, a recently constructed road designed to alleviate the flow of traffic through the town. What a contrast this road makes compared with the lanes of old!

Cross the by-pass via a couple of stiles. Quickly cross another stile and continue along a hedged-in track. Arrive at a junction of tracks. There is a house on the right here. Turn left. After 60 metres the track forks. Go right here and walk along a hedged-in track which shortly turns to the left and gradually descends. After 500 metres there is a joining footpath from the right and a signpost. Continue forward along the hedged-in track in the direction of Beeston Castle and Bulkeley Hill. You have now joined the Sandstone Trail.

The Trail is indicated by way markers—small wooden squares engraved with a footprint containing the letter S, together with a directional arrow.

The hedged-in track terminates. Go over a double stile and footbridge which leads into a field. Keep left along the field edge at first, then forward in the direction of Beeston Castle which can be seen perched on an outcrop of rock, straight ahead. Continue in the general direction of Beeston Castle and cross seven fields and seven stiles to enter a lane.

Leave the Sandstone Trail here and turn left to proceed along the lane. Keep forward for almost ½ mile then pass a row of cottages on the left. The lane starts to climb, but turn left here and cross a stile at the side of a field gate where a footpath sign indicates Tarporley. Continue along a field edge, keeping a hedge on your immediate right. Go over a stile in a crossing fence and quickly negotiate a second stile in a crossing hedge. Climb forward now, aiming towards a telegraph pole, and pass to the right of a facing hedge. Keep forward with a hedge on the left and continue in the direction of the church which can be seen across fields straight ahead. Go over a stile on the left 25 metres before a crossing hedge is arrived at and continue in the same general direction as before, but with a hedge now on the right.

Cross the Tarporley By-pass via a couple of stiles and continue with a hedge now on the left. After a further 120 metres go over a stile on the left which is at the side of a large hawthorn tree. The path keeps parallel with a hedge on the right and leads to a stile in a crossing fence. Go over this stile and walk forward to enter the confines of St Helen's Church.

Retrace your original route back to the car park.

BEESTON CASTLE

WALK 27

★

3½ miles (5.5 km)

OS map 117

This walk commences close to the village of Beeston—which lies 1 mile to the west of the A49 road and is 11 miles north of Whitchurch.

Leave the car in a small car park opposite the entrance of Beeston Castle. (Map ref. 541 591). There is a nominal charge here as the car park is mainly for the use of visitors to the castle, but a visit to the castle is an ideal way to start the walk, as the views from the summit of the crag on which the castle stands are superb.

The castle, built by Rannulf de Blunderville, 7th Earl of Chester, during the early 13th century, played an important role during the Civil War, being captured by the Royalists in 1645. Early the next year, following their eventual victory in the War, the Parliamentarian forces destroyed the greater part of the castle. Although now in ruins, a mental picture can be built up of how it must have looked when in its prime.

On leaving the castle entrance, having explored the ruinous remains, turn right and shortly arrive at the Sandstone Trail car park—which is the place to leave the car if you are not visiting the castle. (Map ref. 540 590).

Follow the trail in the direction of Rawhead and Bickerton. The trail is indicated by way markers—small wooden squares engraved with a footprint containing the letter S, together with a directional arrow. However, you will, initially, only be following the trail for the next 40 metres. The trail forks left through a plantation of conifer trees but keep to the right here to follow a path which skirts around the castle wall. Cross a facing stile and enter a lane. Turn right and shortly pass Castleside Farm on the left. Continue to the Home Farm, then turn right still keeping the castle grounds on the immediate right. This is the most precipitous side of the outcrop of rock on which Beeston Castle stands. Turn next left to enter a lane which is headed by a sign which reads 'Unsuitable for Coaches'.

The lane winds and crosses the railway, then passes over the Shropshire Union Canal by a narrow hump-backed bridge. Keep forward past a quaint waterside inn called the Shady Oak. A T junction is shortly met where the way is right in the direction of Tiverton and Tarporley. Shortly, a lane to Tarporley turns away to the left, but keep forward here in the direction of Tiverton.

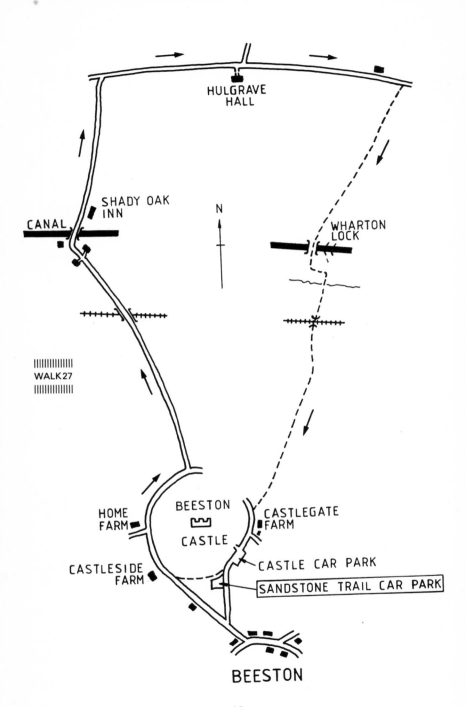

HULGRAVE
HALL

SHADY OAK
INN

CANAL

N

WHARTON
LOCK

WALK 27

BEESTON
CASTLE

HOME
FARM

CASTLEGATE
FARM

CASTLESIDE
FARM

CASTLE CAR PARK

SANDSTONE TRAIL CAR PARK

BEESTON

Opposite this turn-off to Tarporley is Hulgrave Hall, a fine old building which has a large picturesque pond in front of it.

Continue along the lane with fine views across to Beeston Castle on the right. Fifty metres after passing a cottage on the left turn right and cross a stile, where a sign indicates Beeston. You have now re-joined the Sandstone Trail.

Follow the trail over two stiles, then cross a bridge over the canal close to Wharton Lock. The trail continues over the winding river Gowy and enters a tunnel under the railway.

Keep forward over four further stiles to enter a lane, where the way is left. Castlegate Farm is shortly met on the left. The farmhouse is a pleasant black and white building, typical of the older style of Cheshire farms.

Bear to the right and shortly arrive back at the car park.

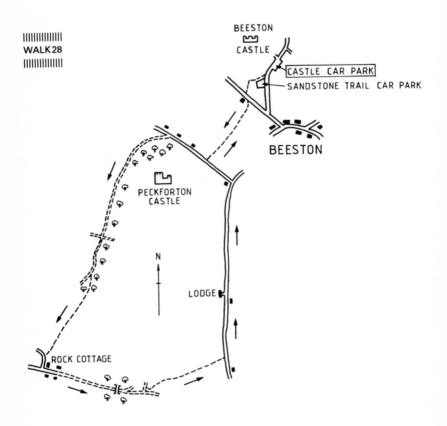

WALK 28

BEESTON
CASTLE

CASTLE CAR PARK
SANDSTONE TRAIL CAR PARK

BEESTON

PECKFORTON
CASTLE

N

LODGE

ROCK COTTAGE

PECKFORTON CASTLE

WALK 28

★

4½ miles (7 km)

OS map 117

Peckforton Castle was built for the first Lord Tollemache during the years 1844 to 1850. It therefore has little historical significance, but nevertheless its outward appearance is all that a castle should be, and its imposing towers and battlements are in complete contrast to the old ruins of Beeston Castle less than a mile away on a facing hilltop.

The walk commences at the Sandstone Trail car park—which is a short distance from the entrance to Beeston Castle. (Map ref. 540 590).

On leaving the car park follow the Sandstone Trail in the direction of Rawhead and Bickerton. The trail is indicated by way markers—small wooden squares engraved with a footprint containing the letter S, together with a directional arrow.

Follow the trail as it skirts around the castle wall and after 40 metres fork left and pass through a small plantation of conifer trees. Cross a stile and enter a lane. Turn left, and then right to enter a field close by a dwelling. Cross the field in the direction of Peckforton Castle, which can be seen straight ahead. Descend steps and cross two stiles. On crossing a further stile enter a lane. Turn right and pass a farm and cottages to where, on the left, the trail joins a wooded track where a sign points towards Bulkeley Hill.

Follow the track as it climbs through the woods and keep forward over a crossing track. The track climbs and leads through a rock cutting, but the trail climbs to the left here to follow a narrow path between trees. On reaching level ground follow the trail through a small wooden gate and emerge from the trees.

Over to the right there are extensive views across the Cheshire Plain.

Cross two stiles and keep forward along a facing lane, then turn left at a T junction close to Rock Cottage. Shortly, the trail turns right over a stile where a sign indicates Bulkeley Hill. Leave the Sandstone Trail here in the direction of Peckforton, and keep forward through a facing gate to follow a sandy track through trees. The track descends. Pass under a bridge and take the second track on the left where a sign indicates Beeston. Almost immediately leave the track to the right and pass along the corner edge of a field to arrive at a stile at the side of a gate. Cross this stile, descend, then cross a second stile to enter a field. Bear diagonally right now to another stile which leads into a large field.

Follow a well-worn path across the field which descends and takes you onto a lane via a further two stiles.

Turn left and follow the lane, passing the lodge gates of Peckforton Castle en route. Turn down the next lane on your left at the side of a dwelling called Park Gate. After 150 metres there is a stile on the right, where a sign indicates Beeston Castle. Cross this stile and retrace your original route back to the car.

RAWHEAD

WALK 29

★

4½ miles (7 km)

OS map 117

Rawhead is aptly named, being an exposed hill open to the full force of the north wind, and warm clothes should be worn if the walk is carried out during the winter months. The outward journey is by way of Peckforton Gap and Bulkeley Hill, where the effort of the initial climb is amply rewarded with superb panoramic views over the surrounding countryside.

The village of Bulkeley lies 8 miles to the north of Whitchurch on the A534 road. Drive in a westerly direction away from the centre of the village and pass The Bickerton Poacher, to arrive at a small parking area on the left hand side of the road opposite Coppermine Lane. (Map ref. 517 542).

On leaving the car, walk back along the A534 to The Bickerton Poacher and fork left to follow a lane in the direction of Beeston and Peckforton. Keep forward for ½ mile to where a footpath sign on the left points towards Peckforton Gap and the Sandstone Trail; this sign is opposite a lane on the right. Bear right here, and follow the path towards Peckforton Gap. The footpath winds between trees then goes straight over a crossing macadam lane. The path crosses a narrow gauge railway track, passes close to storage tanks, then converges with a track from the right. Keep forward and follow the track as it climbs. The track becomes a rocky path. The going is quite steep here. This is Peckforton Gap. The path soon levels out as a lodge gate is met on the right. Turn left here to follow a track where a sign indicates Bulkeley Hill. You have now joined the Sandstone Trail.

The trail is indicated by way markers—small wooden squares engraved with a footprint containing the letter S, together with a directional arrow.

Leave the track after 120 metres and go up steps on the left. Follow the trail as it climbs its rocky way to the top of Bulkeley Hill.

The path continues along virtually level ground, but the hillside on the left drops away quite sharply, and is heavily wooded. Pass the terminus of the narrow gauge railway which you crossed over earlier and arrive at a rock slab from where there are long views over the plains of east Cheshire. Go through a facing iron gateway and follow the trail as it winds through trees. A track is met close to a building. Follow this track as it bends to the left, and shortly emerge from the trees. Go

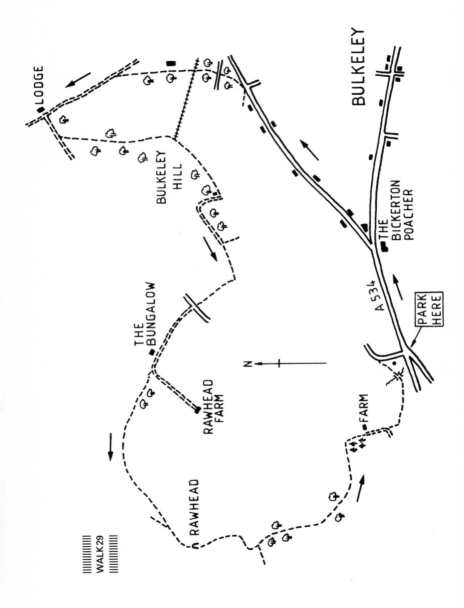

LODGE

BULKELEY

BULKELEY HILL

THE BUNGALOW

RAWHEAD FARM

RAWHEAD

THE BICKERTON POACHER

A 534

PARK HERE

FARM

N

WALK 29

92

through a gap at the side of a field gate and keep forward with an iron fence on your immediate left. After 50 metres the path turns to the right and leads across a field to a stile. Go over this stile, cross Coppermine Lane, and enter a facing track where a sign indicates Rawhead. Keep forward and pass 'The Bungalow'. Shortly, the track turns to the left and leads to Rawhead Farm, but keep forward here to follow a path which takes you over a stile on the left. The path continues, passing rocky outcrops, and leads to steps. Go up the steps and gradually climb for ½ mile, passing over three more stiles, to arrive at the summit of Rawhead.

There is a triangulation station here and the height above sea level is 227 metres. If the day is clear the facing Welsh hills should be visible.

The trail continues and follows a sandstone ridge with a fence and field on the immediate left. Follow the trail as it descends some steps. There is a sheer drop on the right shortly, so please be extremely careful. Continue, then climb again to another fine vantage point. The trail dips and climbs. Pass between birch trees and then keep to the left of a small conifer wood. The path is fenced in on both sides now. Go over a stile close to Chiflik Farm and walk forward down a facing track. After 80 metres the track turns to the right, but keep forward here along a path where a sign points to coppermines. After 30 metres there is a junction of paths. Turn sharp left here and leave the Sandstone Trail to proceed in the direction of the Poacher Inn. The path takes you through banks of gorse. Descend, and cross a footbridge which takes you over a stream, then climb and go over a stile which gives access to a lane.

Turn right and follow the lane as it decends to a T junction, close to where the car is parked.

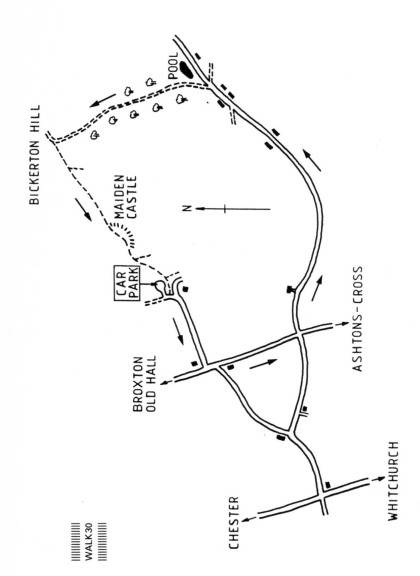

WALK30

BICKERTON HILL

POOL

MAIDEN CASTLE

N

CAR PARK

BROXTON OLD HALL

ASHTONS-CROSS

CHESTER

WHITCHURCH

BICKERTON HILL

WALK 30

★

3 miles (5 km)

OS map 117

Bickerton Hill presents a fine vantage point, offering outstanding views across the Peckforton Hills and Cheshire Plain. Its strategic location was used to advantage by Iron Age man, who built a fortified stronghold close to the cliffs on its north side.

The walk commences close to the village of Duckington, and care has to be exercised in order to find the car park.

The greater part of Duckington village lies between the A41 road and a secondary road which links Broxton Old Hall with Ashtons-Cross. This secondary road runs parallel with the A41 road. Driving through Duckington along this secondary road in the direction of Broxton Old Hall, a thatched cottage is met on the left hand side of the road. A lane at the side of this cottage is headed by a road sign which points to Tilston. Continue for a further 50 metres and turn right to enter a narrow lane which is headed by a no-through-road sign. Drive for 250 metres to arrive at a car park which is surrounded by high banks of earth. (Map ref. 494 526).

Walk down the lane you have just driven up and turn left on meeting the crossing road. Pass the lane which goes to Tilston. Keep forward for 350 metres to arrive at crossroads. Turn left here and walk along a lane in the direction of Bickerton. Follow this typical Cheshire lane as it winds towards Bickerton and arrive at a pool which is on the left hand side of the lane. Leave the lane to the left here to follow a track which goes off to the left just prior to the pool. A sign here points towards Bickerton Hill and the Sandstone Trail. Follow the main track and gradually climb through trees. Continue to where the track turns to the right, but turn to the left here, to join the Sandstone Trail.

The trail is indicated by way markers—small wooden squares engraved with a footprint containing the letter S, together with a directional arrow.

Fork right shortly and climb forward to reach the highest point on the walk at Maiden Castle.

A hill-fort of the Iron Age stood on this exposed site and part of the old earthworks can still be made out. Scientific dating suggests that the hill-fort was occupied around two thousand years ago.

There is a magnificent panorama from here. Over to the right can be seen the wooded outcrop of Rawhead and a little further away the

Peckforton Hills. At the bottom of the hill and to the right, is the village of Brown Knowl. If the day is clear you should be able to make out the waters of the Mersey estuary in the far distance. Further round to the left there are long views into Wales.

From Maiden Castle the trail bears slightly right and descends through trees along a rocky path. Follow the trail as it bears to the left and arrive at a Sandstone Trail information board. You are now only 50 metres from the car.

Continue, and take the next turning right to arrive back at the car park.